First Space Encyclopedia

REVISED EDITION
Editor Ishani Nandi
Assistant editor Debangana Banerjee
Art editor Nehal Verma
Senior editor Shatarupa Chaudhuri
DTP designer Bimlesh Tiwary
Managing editors Laura Gilbert,
Alka Thakur Hazarika
Managing art editors Diane Peyton Jones,
Romi Chakraborty
CTS manager Balwant Singh
Publisher Sarah Larter
Senior producer, pre-production Francesca Wardell
Producer Nicole Landau
Jacket editor Ishani Nandi
Jacket designer Dheeraj Arora
Publishing director Sophie Mitchell
Art director Stuart Jackman
Consultant Carole Stott

ORIGINAL EDITION
Written and edited by Caroline Bingham
Design team Gemma Fletcher, Poppy Joslin,
Sadie Thomas, Mary Sandberg, and Bookwork
Editorial team Carrie Love, Lorrie Mack, and Penny Smith
Publishing manager Susan Leonard
Art Director Rachael Foster
Category Publisher Mary Ling
Picture Researcher Andrea Sadler
DK Picture Library Claire Bowers, Rose Horridge
Production editor Jonathan Ward
Production controller Claire Pearson
Consultant Dr Jon Woodcock

First published in Great Britain in 2008
This edition first published in Great Britain in 2016
by Dorling Kindersley Limited,
80 Strand, London, WC2R 0RL

Copyright © 2008, © 2016
Dorling Kindersley Limited, London
A Penguin Random House Company

4 6 8 10 9 7 5 3 1
001–280447–Jun/2016

All rights reserved. No part of this publication may be
reproduced, stored in a retrieval system, or transmitted
in any form or by any means (electronic, mechanical,
photocopying, recording, or otherwise) without the prior
written permission of the copyright owner.
A CIP catalogue record for this book
is available from the British Library.

ISBN 978-0-24118-874-3

Printed and bound in Hong Kong

A WORLD OF IDEAS:
SEE ALL THERE IS TO KNOW

Lancashire Library Services	
30118134153513	
PETERS	J520BIN
£8.99	31-Mar-2017
CSH	

Contents

What is space?

4-5	What is space?
6-7	Where does space begin?
8-9	Stargazers
10-11	Observatories
12-13	Radio telescopes
14-15	Our place in space
16-17	Great galaxies
18-19	The Milky Way
20-21	Nearby stars
22-23	The Universe

Exploring space

24-25	Exploring space
26-27	Astronaut in training
28-29	What's in your suitcase?
30-31	Rockets
32-33	Moon journey
34-35	Men on the Moon
36-37	Space shuttle
38-39	Space stations
40-41	Living in space
42-43	Working in space
44-45	Artificial satellites
46-47	Exploring Mars
48-49	Reach for the stars!

This book will ask you questions at the bottom of each page...

The solar system
50-51	The solar system
52-53	The Sun
54-55	Eclipse of the Sun
56-57	Mercury
58-59	The morning star
60-61	Third rock from the Sun
62-63	The Moon
64-65	The Red Planet
66-67	King of the planets
68-69	Jupiter's moons
70-71	Saturn
72-73	Distant twins
74-75	Pluto

Comets and meteors
76-77	Comets and meteors
78-79	Just passing
80-81	Shooting stars
82-83	The asteroid belt
84-85	Asteroid landing
86-87	Space debris

Mysteries of space
88-89	Mysteries of space
90-91	UFOs
92-93	Is anyone there?
94-95	Is there life on Mars?
96-97	The Big Bang
98-99	Black holes

100-101	Are there other Earths?
102-103	A star is born
104-105	Death of a star

Space for everyone
106-107	Space for everyone
108-109	Become a stargazer
110-111	Phases of the Moon
112-113	Constellations
114-115	The northern sky
116-117	The southern sky
118-119	Space technology
120-121	Space timeline

Reference section
122-123	True or false?
124-125	Quiz
126-127	Who am I?
128-129	Where in the world?
130-131	Glossary
132-135	Index
136	Picture credits and acknowledgements

About this book
The pages of this book have special features that will show you how to get your hands on as much information as possible! Look out for these:

The Picture detective will get you searching through each section for the answers.

Turn and learn tells you where to look for more information on a subject.

Every page is colour-coded to show you which section it is in.

weird or what?
These buttons give extra weird and wonderful facts about space.

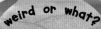

What is space?

Space holds many secrets. It contains places where human beings can be stretched into different shapes, and their body fluids can be boiled, or frozen solid. That's why astronauts wear protective clothing in space. Welcome to the mysterious – and endlessly fascinating – Universe.

What is space?

When people think of space, they think of the following:

 Astronauts feel **weightless** and float around.

 Vast areas of space are **completely empty**.

 Every **star** is a burning ball of gas. Our Sun is a star.

 Astronauts, or **cosmonauts**, are people who travel into space.

 Space probes and **artificial satellites** are what scientists use to explore space.

There is no air in space, so there is **absolute silence**.

A planetary nebula is a colourful cloud of gas and dust ejected by a dying star. This is the Helix Nebula, about 650 light years away, seen from NASA's Spitzer Space Telescope.

Is that space?

On a cloudless night, you can see thousands of stars. Space is the name we give to the huge empty areas in between the atmospheres of stars and planets. Apart from the odd rock, space is sprinkled only with dust and gas.

Too big to imagine

Astronomers measure distance in space in light years. One light year is the distance light travels in one year – that's about 10 million million km (6 million million miles).

4

Why is space so dark?

Space is dark because there is nothing there to reflect light. From space, the Earth looks lit up because light from our Sun reflects off sea and land, and the particles in our atmosphere.

US astronaut Michael Gernhardt went on four separate space missions, and spent more than 23 hours walking around in space.

Picture detective

Look through the What is Space? section and see if you can identify the pictures below.

Turn and learn

Searching for a star: **pp. 48-49**
Living in space: **pp. 40-41**

Experts believe it's just under 14 billion years old.

5

Where does space begin?

The Earth is cloaked in a thin layer of gases – the atmosphere. Outside this atmosphere is space, where there is no air to breathe, or to allow wings to fly, and where nobody can hear you scream.

Fading away

Our atmosphere does not just end suddenly – it fades gradually into space.

View from Mir

The Russian Mir space station was in orbit for 15 years. Here, it was photographed by the US shuttle *Atlantis*.

EXOSPHERE

The exosphere is the outer layer of the atmosphere, extending about 10,000 km (6,000 miles) above the ground. From here, lighter gases drift into space beyond.

THERMOSPHERE

The thermosphere reaches way up to more than 700 km (over 400 miles) above the Earth. The polar lights (aurora borealis in the north and aurora australis in the south) glow in the thermosphere.

Most experts agree that space begins at 100 km (63 miles) above the ground. Past this, our image is not drawn to scale.

MESOSPHERE

The mesosphere extends about 85 km (53 miles) above the ground. The air is thin here, but it's still thick enough to slow meteorites down.

STRATOSPHERE

The stratosphere rises about 50 km (31 miles) above the Earth. Planes cruise in the upper troposphere or lower stratosphere, above the clouds.

TROPOSPHERE

The troposphere extends between 6 and 20 km (3½–12 miles) above the ground. All our weather takes place in the troposphere.

What is the mix of gases that makes up our atmosphere called?

Space badge

The US space agency NASA (National Aeronautics and Space Administration) awards astronaut wings to service personnel and civilians who have flown more than 80 km (50 miles) above the Earth's surface. Shown here are civilian astronaut wings.

If you could drive a car straight up, it would take only about an hour to reach space.

Gaia, a European satellite, launched in 2013

Fuel tank

Rocket booster

Orbiter

The parts of a spacecraft (the orbiter, fuel tank, and rocket boosters) are streamlined for lift-off.

Slipping through air

A spacecraft has to be streamlined to move easily and safely through air. Where necessary, an extra part, called a fairing, is added to achieve this effect. A nose cone – the front end of a rocket, or aircraft – is an example of a fairing.

Space hat-ellite

Up in space, satellites can be any shape at all. They don't need to be streamlined, because there's no air there.

7

Stargazers

People have studied celestial objects for thousands of years. This study is called astronomy. Around 400 years ago, a special tool was invented that made the task easier – this tool is called a telescope.

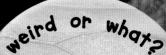

weird or what?
Galileo's discoveries were not welcomed by the Church in 17th-century Italy, and he spent the last few years of his life under house arrest.

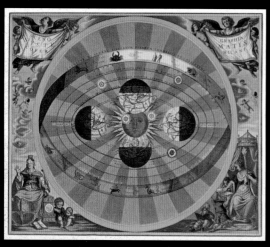

Copernicus placed the Sun at the centre of the planets. He "stopped the Sun and moved the Earth".

Before the telescope
People were shocked when Polish astronomer Nicolaus Copernicus suggested in 1543 that the Earth was just another planet and the planets orbited (went around) the Sun. Then, it was a common belief that the Earth was at the centre of the Universe.

Guess what I can see!
The Italian astronomer Galileo Galilei built a simple telescope in 1609 and proved Copernicus had been right. He discovered Venus had phases (like our Moon), he saw Jupiter's moons, and he spotted mountains on our Moon.

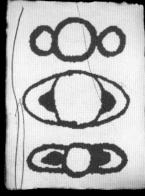

Saturn as sketched by Galileo – he thought Saturn's rings were two moons or "ears".

Replica of a 17th-century telescope

Saturn as we know it today

8

Hubble has taken incredibly detailed images, such as this one of the death of a star.

Hubble is monitored by the Flight Operations Team (FOT) at the Goddard Space Flight Center in Greenbelt, Maryland, USA. The team use computers to constantly check all is running well.

The Hubble Telescope was designed in the 20th century.

Hubble is about the size of a school bus.

Antenna used for sending and receiving signals from the Earth

Solar panels convert sunlight into electricity.

An eye in space

Now we have telescopes in space, most famously the Hubble Space Telescope (HST). It orbits the Earth at a speed of around 28,000 kph (17,400 mph) and is controlled from the Earth.

The James Webb Space Telescope (JWST) is currently being planned to replace Hubble in 2018. It will see farther and more clearly than Hubble.

Many people credit spectacle-maker Hans Lippershey with its invention in 1608.

Observatories

Light is constantly reaching us from space, and one way astronomers learn about space is by studying this light. To do this effectively, an astronomer needs a telescope and a clear night sky.

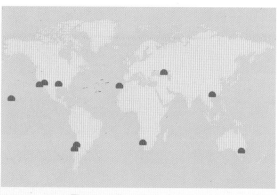

The world's major observatories are all on extinct volcanoes or high mountains, as this is where the air is clearest.

Island observatory

Two of the world's largest light-detecting telescopes are the twin Keck telescopes. These are on the summit of Mauna Kea, a dormant (sleeping) volcano in Hawaii. The summit is clear of light and dust pollution. They both contain mirrors that are 10 m (33 ft) across.

Twin Keck telescopes

From how far away can the Chandra spot something as small as a road sign?

A better view

The Royal Greenwich Observatory moved its telescopes three times because pollution clouded their view. Originally in Greenwich, near London, England, the telescopes ended up in the Canary Islands, 2.3 km (1.4 miles) above sea level.

Space telescope

Scientists use the Chandra X-ray Observatory telescope to study black holes and exploding stars.

A "Finderscope" is used to line up the main telescope.

What's in a name?

A telescope with a lens or mirror, called an optical telescope, gathers more light than the human eye. Large telescopes use mirrors – the larger the mirror, the more it can see. Telescope projects are often given grand names – the Very Large Telescope, the European Extremely Large Telescope, and the Overwhelmingly Large Telescope (which is yet to be built).

Near to the twin Keck telescopes are the Canada-France-Hawaii Telescope and Gemini North telescope.

Large mirror inside

From up to 20 km (12 miles).

Radio telescopes

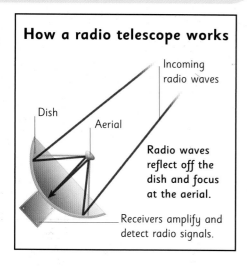

How a radio telescope works

Incoming radio waves

Dish

Aerial

Radio waves reflect off the dish and focus at the aerial.

Receivers amplify and detect radio signals.

Invisible radio waves surround us. They also reach us from space, and large dishes are used to pick them up, day and night, to help astronomers learn more about space.

So do the dishes "listen" to space?

No. Radio astronomers do not listen to noises. Sound waves do not pass through space. The dishes pick up radio waves, a receiver measures them, and a computer turns this information into a picture.

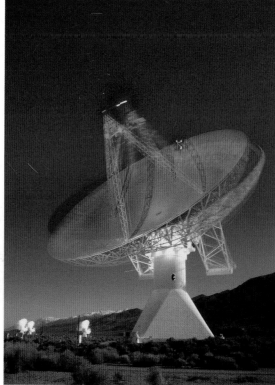

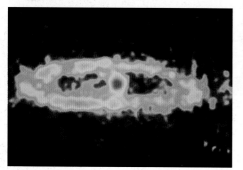

Radio telescope image of the Andromeda Galaxy. The red centre is producing the strongest signals.

Tilt and learn

Radio dishes are designed to tilt and move around, so radio astronomers can point them at the bit of space they want to study. Also, as the Earth turns, radio dishes need to move in order to follow one spot in the sky. The movements, which are controlled by computer, are very precise.

No mountain in sight!

Unlike optical telescopes, radio telescopes don't need to be built at the top of mountains, as radio waves will pass through cloud cover. Each dish reflects and focuses the incoming radio signals onto an aerial mounted above it. The dishes can be enormous.

Can you name some of the everyday uses of radio waves, apart from for radios?

Big in every way

The Very Large Array (VLA) in New Mexico has 27 dishes, each 5 m (82 ft) in diameter. Used individually or together to sweep the sky for signals, they rest on tracks and can be spread over 36 km (22 miles)!

Astronomers didn't discover radio waves from space until 1932.

People need to get inside the dishes to carry out repairs and maintenance.

did you know?
Diesel cars are used near radio observatories, as the spark plugs in petrol-powered cars can create radio waves that interfere with the ones from space.

13

Our place in space

The Earth seems huge to us – after all, it can take you a long time just to travel to school! But the Earth is only a very tiny part of space. So where exactly does it belong in the Universe?

The Earth looks like a swirly blue marble suspended in space.

The Earth and its moon

The Earth, our home in space, has one natural satellite – the Moon. It is about one quarter of the size of the Earth and, on average, orbits about 384,000 km (240,000 miles) away from us.

Saturn

Jupiter

Uranus

Earth

Venus

Mercury

Mars

Neptune

Astronauts, who have seen the Earth from space, are struck by its beauty. One described it as looking like a Christmas-tree decoration.

This picture shows where the planets are located. None of them, or their orbits, are drawn to scale.

The solar system

The Earth is the third planet from the Sun, at just the right distance from it to support life. The eight planets that orbit the Sun (plus moons, comets, asteroids, meteoroids, dwarf planets, dust, and gas) make up our solar system.

Which was the ninth planet of the solar system, now classed as a dwarf planet?

In a spin

Our galaxy has long curved arms that spiral out from a central bulge.

The Milky Way

The Local Group

The Milky Way is one of the largest galaxies in a cluster known as the Local Group. Millions of galaxy clusters make up the Universe.

Our Sun and the solar system

The Milky Way

Our solar system is located in a galaxy called the Milky Way, a collection of billions of stars. It lies on the edge of one of the spiral arms.

Our home in space supports trillions of living things.

Pluto.

Great galaxies

A galaxy is a family of stars, gas, and dust held together by gravity. Much of a galaxy is empty space, with distances between each star that are hard to imagine.

Many galaxies are found in galaxy clusters, with thousands of members. Our galaxy, the Milky Way, belongs to a cluster of more than 50 galaxies called the Local Group.

Two galaxies may sometimes collide. This image shows two spiral galaxies that have moved together.

A guide to galaxies

Galaxies differ enormously in size, shape, and mass, but they do fall into a basic pattern, depending on their shape (though we don't know what gives them a particular shape!).

Spiral galaxies

These disc-shaped galaxies spin slowly. They look a bit like whirlpools, and often have two arms that curl out from a central bulge. The Messier 74 is an example of a spiral galaxy.

Barred spiral galaxies

Barred spiral galaxies have arms that wind out from the ends of a central bar of stars rather than from the core. The Milky Way is an example of a barred spiral galaxy.

Why are some galaxies named by letters and numbers?

get mucky

Paint your own galaxy with white paint on black paper. Then splash drops of paint onto the paper to represent stars.

Collision course

Two galaxies may collide in a process that will take millions of years. The stars within the galaxy won't collide, but the gas and dust will – this collision can create new stars.

Elliptical galaxies

These galaxies are shaped like balls or eggs and are largely made up of old stars. They don't contain the gas clouds for the formation of new stars. An example of an elliptical galaxy is M87.

Irregular galaxies

Irregular galaxies of this kind have no shape. They contain lots of gas and dust, and many are therefore active nurseries for the formation of new stars. The UGC 8201 is an example of an irregular galaxy.

17

Because there are so many. The names are codes that act like barcode numbers.

The Milky Way

Our solar system is a tiny part of a gigantic barred spiral galaxy, the Milky Way. This is made up of billions of stars, which look as if they have been sprinkled thickly onto the night sky.

Scientists think there are about 400,000 million stars in the Milky Way galaxy, but there may be even more.

Why is it milky?

Before the invention of telescopes, people could not see the stars very clearly – they were blurred together in a hazy white streak. The ancient Greeks called this streak a "river of milk". This is how our galaxy became known as the Milky Way.

Turn and learn

Stargazers:
pp. 8-9
Our solar system:
pp. 50-51

Milky myths

Many myths have developed about the formation of the Milky Way.

Native American stories tell of a dog dropping corn as he fled across the sky.

Kalahari bushmen say it was created by hot embers thrown up from a fire.

Hindu myth sees the milkiness as the speckled belly of a dolphin.

The **ancient Egyptians** believed the stars were a pool of cow's milk.

A side view

The Milky Way, like all spiral and barred spiral galaxies, is flat, with a bulge at the centre, and arms that circle outwards.

Where are the oldest stars in the Milky Way?

The time it takes for our solar system to orbit the Milky Way once is known as a galactic year. It is approximately 230 million years.

We are here!

It takes light 100,000 years to pass from one edge of the Milky Way to the other.

In a sphere of stars surrounding the galaxy, often in giant balls called globular clusters.

Nearby stars

Our nearest star is the Sun. It seems a very long way away, yet the Sun's light takes just over eight minutes to reach us. The light from our next-nearest star, Proxima Centauri, doesn't get to the Earth for more than four years.

The Sun contains 99.8 per cent of the total mass of the solar system.

The Earth

Light years away

Astronomers measure space distance in light years, because the distances are so great that normal measurements have little meaning. A light year is the distance light travels in a year.

How far is Proxima Centauri from the Earth?

Why do stars twinkle?

Stars twinkle because of movements in the Earth's atmosphere. Starlight enters the atmosphere as straight rays, but air moves the light's path so it appears to flicker or "twinkle".

Proxima Centauri

Proxima Centauri was only discovered in 1915. It's very faint, so it can't be seen without the aid of a telescope. It looks red because it's a red dwarf star.

Proxima Centauri

We don't know whether Proxima Centauri has planets or not. This artist's impression shows what the view from one of its planets might look like.

Nearest neighbours

Proxima Centauri lies in a group of three stars called Alpha Centauri. The others are Alpha Centauri A and Alpha Centauri B, which are both like our Sun, so experts believe they may have planets that support life.

Almost 40 trillion km (25 trillion miles).

The Universe

A typical galaxy contains over 100,000 million stars.

The Universe includes the Earth and its moon, the Sun and the solar system, the Milky Way, the galaxies we know, and the galaxies we haven't yet discovered.

That's big...
The galaxies are spread over such unimaginable distances that even a space probe would take two billion years to cross our galaxy.

... and getting bigger
The Universe is still expanding, so all the galaxies are moving farther and farther apart.

How fast does the space probe *Voyager 1* travel?

Dark mysteries

We can't see everything in space. Experts think there's lots of mysterious "dark matter" between the stars.

hands on

Make your own Universe by drawing dots and spirals around a flat balloon to represent galaxies. As you blow air in, these "galaxies" move apart — that's what's happening to the Universe.

More of the same?

There might be other, parallel, Universes — experts call these the "multiverse".

Exploring space

When you're trying to imagine the vastness of space, consider that *Voyager 1*, which was launched in 1977, has just travelled out of our solar system. A new era of space exploration has begun.

Saturn

The communications dish, which doubles as a sunshade to prevent overheating

Astronaut Leroy Chiao

By any other name

The word astronaut comes from two Greek words – *astron*, meaning "star" and *nautes*, meaning "sailor". Russian astronauts are called cosmonauts (from the Greek words *kosmos*, meaning "universe", and *nautes*). Chinese astronauts are called *yuhangyuan* – literally "universe travel worker" or "space navigator".

Cosmonaut Yuri Malenchenko

24

How long did it take *Cassini-Huygens* to reach Saturn?

As the crow flies?

Spacecraft launched from the Earth do not necessarily travel to their destination in a straight line. The *Cassini-Huygens* orbiter and probe, for example, took a roundabout route during its mission to Saturn in order to make use of gravity assists (see below).

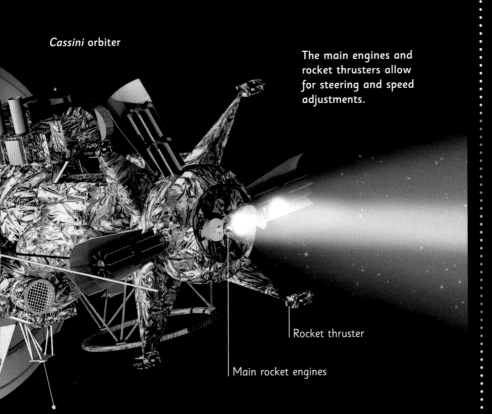

Cassini orbiter

The main engines and rocket thrusters allow for steering and speed adjustments.

Rocket thruster

Main rocket engines

Picture detective

Look through the Exploring Space section and see if you can identify the pictures below.

What is a gravity assist?

By flying past a planet and making use of its gravity to change speed and direction, a gravity assist helps spacecraft on their way. *Cassini-Huygens* travelled twice past Venus, once past the Earth, and once past Jupiter before it headed for Saturn.

Turn and learn

Rockets: **pp. 30-31** Space stations: **pp. 38-39**

Almost seven years.

Astronaut in training

Astronauts do not just climb into a spacecraft and zip off into space – they need months of study and training first. They have to be in peak physical condition, and some astronauts claim their training is much harder than any mission.

Whatever it takes

Astronauts train for all sorts of situations. When necessary, they use real aircraft, equipment simulators, virtual reality systems, and computer simulations. A simulator imitates a situation or environment that an astronaut can be trained in before experiencing the real environment.

Underwater training

Floating in water is very much like floating in space, so astronauts use special water tanks to train for space walks. One NASA tank can hold full-size modules of the International Space Station.

During an exercise, five NASA astronauts-in-training pull an "injured" crewmate to safety after a simulated parachute jump.

26

Around and around

A multi-axis trainer helps astronauts get used to the out-of-control spinning feeling they'll get from tumbling in weightless conditions.

Walking on the Moon

In the 1960s, Apollo mission astronauts would practice moon-walking by moving along a wall while suspended at an angle by heavy cables. Such training took place at NASA's Lunar Landing Research Facility in Virginia, USA in a Reduced Gravity Walking Simulator, such as the one here.

Weightless wonder

Flown in a special way, an aeroplane with no seats and padded walls helps astronauts get used to feeling weightless. This plane is known as the "vomit comet" because its motion makes people feel sick.

27

Astronauts have two years of basic training, plus advanced training for missions.

What's in your suitcase?

Just like you pack to go on holiday, astronauts pack lots of things to take into space. They wear different clothes depending on what they are doing.

Launch Entry Suit

Ready to go

During launch and re-entry, astronauts wear a special bright-orange suit, called a Launch Entry Suit, or "pumpkin suit". Tools are stored in huge pockets on the legs.

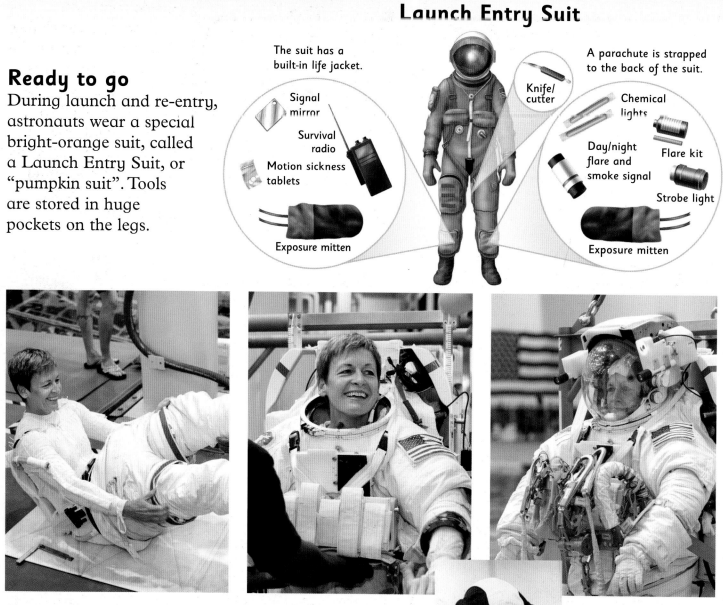

The suit has a built-in life jacket.

Signal mirror

Survival radio

Motion sickness tablets

Exposure mitten

Knife/ cutter

A parachute is strapped to the back of the suit.

Chemical lights

Day/night flare and smoke signal

Flare kit

Strobe light

Exposure mitten

A peek underneath

For a spacewalk, astronauts need to wear an extravehicular mobility unit, or EMU. Underneath this, astronauts wear space underwear, a one-piece suit with small, water-carrying tubes that help keep them cool.

Under the helmet, there's a communications cap, called a "Snoopy" cap, that has a headphone and microphone.

Can you guess how long an EMU can support an astronaut working in space?

A safe journey
Astronauts carry safety equipment in case of emergency.

 Life rafts are used if the crew have to crash land at sea.

 Sea dye is used to colour water after an emergency landing to alert rescuers.

Astronauts must **drink** fluids regularly to prevent dehydration.

 Astronauts carry **chemical lightsticks** with them in the pocket of their suit.

Chill-out time
Inside their craft, astronauts wear clothes they would wear on the Earth, such as shorts and a T-shirt. Clothes are not changed as often as they would be on the Earth – after all, there are no washing machines on board a space station!

Just popping out
Extravehicular mobility units, or EMUs, are a bit like miniature spaceships. They provide astronauts with all they need to survive. They are used for working outside a spacecraft such as the International Space Station.

An astronaut needs to work outside to repair satellites, or check the outside of the spacecraft.

For about 8½ hours.

Rockets

Rockets carry satellites and people into space. A rocket burns fuel to produce a jet of gas. The hot gas expands rapidly and is blasted downwards causing a force (the thrust) to push the rocket up.

A nose cone, or fairing, reduces air resistance as the rocket takes off.

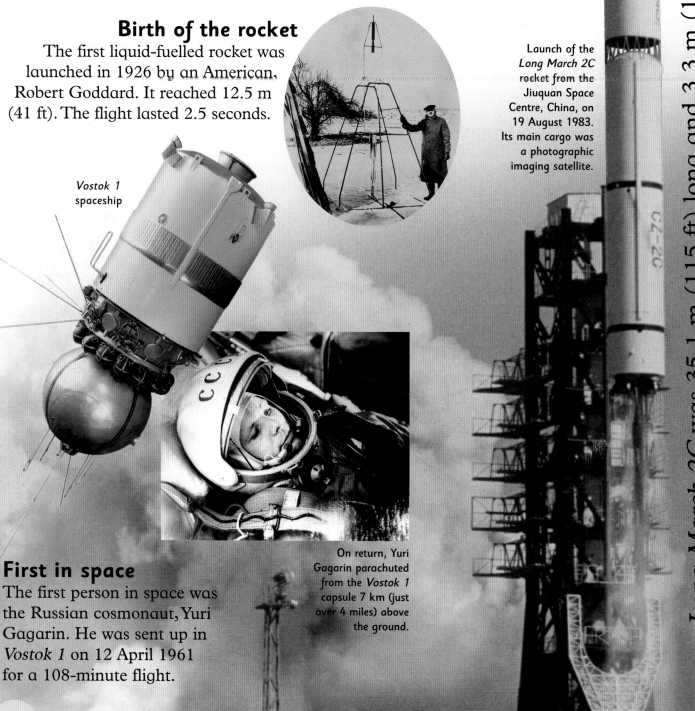

Birth of the rocket
The first liquid-fuelled rocket was launched in 1926 by an American, Robert Goddard. It reached 12.5 m (41 ft). The flight lasted 2.5 seconds.

Vostok 1 spaceship

Launch of the *Long March 2C* rocket from the Jiuquan Space Centre, China, on 19 August 1983. Its main cargo was a photographic imaging satellite.

On return, Yuri Gagarin parachuted from the *Vostok 1* capsule 7 km (just over 4 miles) above the ground.

Long March 2C was 35.1 m (115 ft) long and 3.3 m (11 ft) wide.

First in space
The first person in space was the Russian cosmonaut, Yuri Gagarin. He was sent up in *Vostok 1* on 12 April 1961 for a 108-minute flight.

How many tests were needed for the engine that powered the first stage of *Ariane 5*?

To escape the Earth's gravity, a rocket has to reach just over 11 km (7 miles) per second. This is called the escape velocity.

Types of rocket
There are many different kinds of rocket.

 Soyuz rockets are used by astronauts to reach the International Space Station.

 Saturn V were the largest rockets ever built. They were used to launch all the Moon landings.

 Firework rockets are used for celebrations.

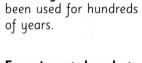 **Military rockets** have been used for hundreds of years.

 Experimental rockets provide information about fast and high flight.

 Some satellites have small rocket engines to position them once they are in orbit.

Regular launches
Today, rockets such as *Ariane 5* are used to launch satellites into space. A satellite is a rocket's payload, or cargo, whose size determines whether it is sent up by a small or large rocket.

This is the *Ariane 5* launch vehicle. The main tank contains 25 tonnes (27.5 tons) of liquid hydrogen. The tubes on each side are solid fuel boosters that supply extra power for lift-off.

Biggest and best
The *Saturn V* were the largest, and most powerful, rockets ever built. They were used 13 times, between 1967 and 1973, including for the first Moon landing.

Around 300 tests were done.

Moon journey

During the 1960s there was a race between the USA and the former Soviet Union to put a human on the Moon. The USA succeeded by landing the first humans on the Moon with *Apollo 11* in 1969.

Apollo 11 reached the Moon because of a huge rocket called *Saturn V*. Most of *Saturn V* contained the fuel needed to blast it into space. Three astronauts sat in a tiny capsule at the top of the rocket.

10 The service module is ejected before re-entry into the Earth's atmosphere.

Service and command modules **9**

The journey back

1 Five F1 engines blast the *Saturn V* rocket into space from the Kennedy Space Center.

11 The command module is the only part of the mission to return to the Earth.

Earth

Kennedy Space Center

The journey out

12
Command module

13
Re-entering atmosphere

3 The command and service modules separate from the rocket and perform a 180° turn.

2 The rocket's engines fire to set the craft on a course to the Moon.

The service module contained the power and life-support systems.

What was Apollo 11?
Apollo 11 was the first manned mission to land on the Moon. It was made up of three modules, or parts: the tiny command module, the service module, and the lunar module.

How many astronauts have walked on the Moon?

Turn and learn
The first Moon landing:
pp. 34-35
Rockets:
pp. 30-31

5 The rest of the rocket is discarded while the command, service, and lunar modules continue to the Moon.

6 The journey has taken 102 hours, 45 minutes. The lunar module is ready to land.

7 The command and service modules orbit the Moon (one astronaut remains on board) while the lunar module lands. Two astronauts walk on the Moon.

Moon

8 The lunar module joins the command and service modules so the two lunar astronauts can climb through. The lunar module is then abandoned.

4 The command and service modules reattach to the lunar module, which is still connected to the rocket.

The Eagle has landed
The lunar module (the part of *Apollo 11* that landed) was also known as the *Eagle*. It touched down on the surface of the Moon on 20 July 1969.

The three astronauts worked and slept in the command module.

Apollo 11

Mission commander Neil Armstrong struggled to find a flat landing site. He succeeded with just seconds to spare.

Men on the Moon

On 20 July 1969, Neil Armstrong became the first person to walk on the surface of the Moon. He was joined by Buzz Aldrin. A third astronaut, Michael Collins, remained in orbit with the command and service modules.

weird or what? The lunar module computer on *Apollo 11* had approximately 64KB of memory. Some calculators can now store more than 500KB.

The lunar module was nicknamed the *Eagle*.

What did they do?
Armstrong and Aldrin spent almost 22 hours on the Moon. About 2.5 hours of this was spent outside the *Eagle*, collecting rock and soil samples, setting up experiments, and taking pictures.

What was it like?
Buzz Aldrin described the Moon's surface as like nothing on Earth. He said it consisted of a fine, talcum-powder-like dust, strewn with pebbles and rocks.

Why is there no blue sky on the Moon?

Here comes the Earth

Instead of the Moon rising, the astronauts saw the Earth rising over the Moon's horizon – it looked four times bigger than the Moon looks from the Earth.

How did they talk?

There's no air in space, so sound has nothing to travel through. Lunar astronauts use radio equipment in their helmets to talk to each other.

Neil Armstrong

We have transport!

Three later Apollo missions each carried a small electric car, a lunar rover, which allowed the astronauts to explore away from the lander. These were left on the Moon when the astronauts left.

This dish antennae allowed the astronauts to send pictures to the Earth.

One lunar rover reached a top speed of 22 kph (13.5 mph).

Splashdown

The astronauts returned to the Earth in the *Apollo 11* command module. This fell through the atmosphere and landed in the Pacific Ocean. A ringed float helped to keep it stable.

35

Because the Moon has no atmosphere.

Space shuttle

NASA's space shuttle programme was first launched in April 1981, and completed its last mission in 2011. The partly reusable craft taught astronauts an immense amount about working in space.

Ditch the tanks!
The rocket boosters were released two minutes after launch. They parachuted back to the Earth and would be used again. The tank was discarded eight minutes after launch, and broke up in the atmosphere.

Which bit is that?
The shuttle had three main components – the orbiter (the plane part, and the only part that went into orbit), a huge fuel tank, and two rocket boosters.

Heat protection
Nearly 25,000 heat-resistant tiles covered the orbiter to protect it from high temperatures on re-entry.

Main (external) fuel tank

The orbiter carried between five and seven crew members.

Discovery

There were two rocket boosters, one on each side. Once lit, the boosters could not be shut off. They burned until they ran out of fuel.

The orbiter's engines were used once the orbiter reached space.

weird or what?
Woodpeckers delayed a space shuttle launch in 1995 by pecking holes in the fuel tank's insulating foam. Plastic owls were later used to frighten other birds away.

How long did it take the orbiter to reach space?

Pop it in there!

Each orbiter had a huge payload bay. You could park a school bus in this cavity, which held the satellites, experiments, and laboratories that needed to be taken into space.

The payload's doors opened once the shuttle was in orbit.

The orbiter fleet

Five orbiters were built. Two have been lost in tragic accidents.

Columbia first flew in 1981. It disintegrated on re-entry in 2003.

Challenger was destroyed in 1986, just 73 seconds after launch.

Discovery first flew in 1984. It marked the 100th shuttle mission in 2000.

Atlantis first flew in 1985. It completed 33 missions, the last one in 2011.

Endeavour replaced *Challenger*. It flew 25 missions between 1992 and 2011.

Space shuttle *Endeavour* landing at Edwards Air Force Base, California, USA.

A safe landing

Shuttles glided down, belly first. Once the orbiter touched the runway, it released a 12-m (40-ft) drag chute to slow it down.

The future explorer

NASA tested a new orbiter, called the *Orion Multipurpose Crew Vehicle*, on 5 December 2014. It is designed to carry six astronauts on each mission, the first of which is planned for the 2020s. This will make it possible for humans to explore asteroids and Mars.

The *Orion Multipurpose Crew Vehicle*

It took just over eight minutes.

Space stations

Imagine living more than 380 km (235 miles) above everyone else, experiencing a sunrise or sunset every 45 minutes, sending your clothes to be burned up in the atmosphere rather than washed, and having no floor or ceiling. Welcome to life on a space station.

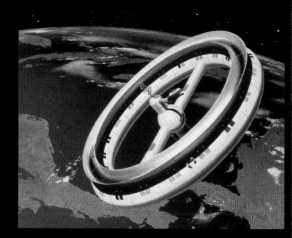

First ideas

Ideas for space stations existed a long time before they became a reality. In the 1950s, the space scientist Wernher von Braun proposed a wheel-shaped design that was 76 m (250 ft) wide.

Space stations

There have been 11 space stations since 1971. They include the following.

 Salyut 1 was launched in 1971, and was in orbit for 175 days (of which 24 were occupied).

 Salyut 7 was launched in 1982. It was in orbit for 3,216 days (of which 816 were manned).

 Skylab, launched in May 1973 by the USA, burned up in 1979.

 Mir was built in space by the Soviet Union, beginning in 1986. It fell into the atmosphere in March 2001.

A quick history

The first space station, Salyut 1, was launched in 1971. Since then, a number of stations have orbited the Earth. The International Space Station (ISS), launched in 1998, has been built by 15 nations working together. The largest space station ever built, it's been occupied since 2000. This picture of the ISS was taken in 2005, in mid-build.

What is a space station?

It's a space laboratory that orbits the Earth, operated by crews of astronauts who take turns living and working on it. Each crew stays for several weeks or months. Occasionally, an astronaut has stayed a whole year!

The ISS is constantly growing, as new parts are added. This photograph was taken in 2010.

The ISS has been put together in space, from modules (parts of a spacecraft that can also work on their own).

Solar panels are used to power the space station.

Crews of astronauts are brought to the ISS on a Russian *Soyuz* spacecraft.

Zarya control module

Zvezda service module

39

Living in space

A bed on the wall, baby wipes for a wash, footholds, and edible toothpaste! Life on a space station is very different from life on the Earth.

Ordinary days

Astronauts need to do everything that you do. They eat, exercise, sleep, work, and play, but they have to do all these things in a home without gravity.

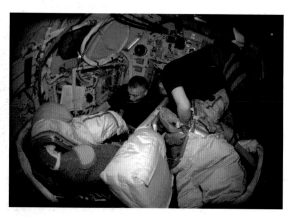

It's not easy to sort out bulky spacesuits in weightlessness!

New arrivals

When astronauts arrive at a space station, they bring supplies with them. Imagine trying to unpack your suitcase when you are floating!

weird or what?

Some astronauts suffer temporary hearing problems after living on a space station. Why? Because the necessary air filters, fans, and pumps make it VERY NOISY!

Keeping fit

Astronauts' muscles don't work very hard in weightlessness, so they quickly lose strength. Hence, astronauts exercise for about two hours a day. This astronaut completed a marathon on the International Space Station treadmill.

What were the first living things to be launched into space?

Time for work

Some astronauts carry out a variety of experiments and record the results, while others do spacewalks to help construct the space station.

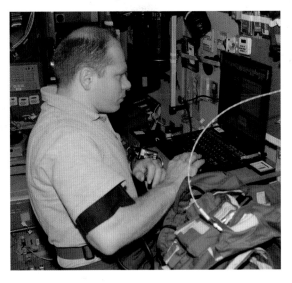

A tasty lunch?

Food is supplied in sealed packets and some of it is dehydrated. That means that water has to be added before the food can be eaten.

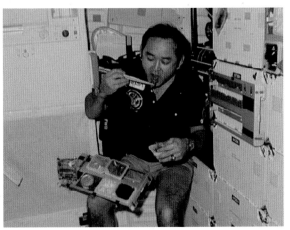

Time for bed

Most of the crew use sleeping bags, which have to be strapped to the walls of the space station. The bag holds astronauts' arms in place. Otherwise they would float about.

We like to keep clean, too!

Astronauts use combs, toothbrushes, and toothpaste. But the toothpaste doesn't froth, and gets swallowed. Wet wipes are useful for a speedy wash.

Hair washing is possible, but rare.

They were fruit flies, launched on 20 February 1947, by the USA.

Working in space

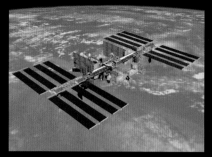
International Space Station (ISS)

We have all seen workers on a construction site, hammering and drilling. Imagine a construction site travelling in space high above the Earth's surface. That's what astronauts have to cope with when they are repairing a satellite, or putting together a space station.

Illustration of how a sunrise would look from space

Is it warm today?
In orbit, the strong sunshine heats astronauts up. Surprisingly, it's difficult to lose heat in space, so spacesuits have to include a refrigeration unit!

An astronaut may be outside the space station for hours at a time. This one is working on the station's robotic arm.

Between 1998 and 2015, more than 360 spacewalks were performed by astronauts outside the International Space Station. Two astronauts always spacewalk together on the ISS.

hands on
Astronauts say that moving their hands in their gloves is difficult. To feel what they mean, put a rubber band around your closed fingers and try to open them. Do this 15 times.

What does EVA stand for?

A piece of history

The first-ever spacewalk was performed by Soviet astronaut Alexei Leonov on 18 March 1965. He was soon followed by American Edward White on 3 June 1965.

Edward White was the first American to spacewalk.

Alexei Leonov became a celebrity in the Soviet Union and around the world.

Slow down

Astronauts have to work slower than construction workers on the Earth. If they twist a bolt too quickly, they will send themselves into a spin.

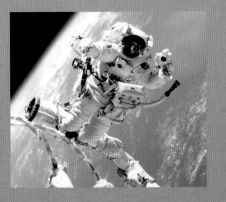

Make it larger

Space tools are extra large so that astronauts can grab them in their bulky gloves. They also have to be tied to the astronaut to prevent them from floating away.

Extra Vehicular Activity. It means spacewalking!

Artificial satellites

A satellite is an object, natural or man-made, that orbits something bigger than itself. The Moon is the Earth's natural satellite, but thousands of man-made satellites are currently orbiting our Earth as well.

The word "satellite" comes from the Latin word for "attendant".

This satellite didn't work because a launch problem left it too close to the Earth. Space-walking shuttle astronauts fitted a rocket motor to boost it into the correct orbit.

The *Telstar* satellite relayed the first satellite television signal in 1962.

Domestic satellite dishes receive the signals sent by television satellites.

Space litter

Of the thousands of artificial satellites currently orbiting the Earth, many are no longer working. Bits and parts that have fallen off other satellites or rockets are also floating around in space.

44

What was the first artificial satellite called?

Large bowl-shaped antennae send and receive signals from satellites orbiting the Earth. These antennae can be turned to track a satellite as it moves across the sky.

Charging up

Many satellites have huge solar panels that collect the Sun's rays. These make electricity to recharge on-board batteries that power the satellite.

What do they do?

Most artificial satellites are communication satellites, used for things like telephone calls, live television broadcasts, and computer link-ups. Other satellites help with a variety of different jobs, from guiding aeroplanes and ships to weather forecasting.

Weather satellites take pictures of the Earth to show the type and location of clouds, and to measure land and sea temperatures. This is a hurricane moving across the ocean.

Satellite catalogue

There are many different types of satellite.

 Communications satellites capture radio signals and send them to different places in the world. They help us to keep in touch.

 Resource satellites take pictures of natural resources on the Earth. These are sent to scientists, who turn them into maps of things such as oil deposits.

 Navigation satellites are used by pilots and sailors to help them work out their location. In case of emergency, they can also pick up distress signals.

 Military satellites are used by the armed forces for navigation, communication, and monitoring by taking pictures and intercepting radio waves.

 Scientific satellites help experts to study the planets, the Sun, other solar systems, and things like asteroids, comets, and black holes.

 Weather satellites help scientists to study weather. Like resource satellites, they have cameras, and they work in a similar way.

It was called *Sputnik 1*. It was launched by the Soviet Union on 4 October 1957.

Exploring Mars

Spacecraft have flown past Mars, orbited it, and landed on its surface. One day, we may even build a base on Mars. It may be cold, barren, and dusty, but it's full of possibilities.

Why study Mars?

At some point in its history, Mars, also called the Red Planet, may have supported life forms. Although it is about half the size of the Earth, it has clouds, weather patterns, and polar icecaps – once it even had active volcanoes. Learning about Mars may help us to understand our own planet.

On the barren surface of Mars, the robotic *Sojourner* rover examines a rock later nicknamed "Yogi".

Seeing red

The landing craft that visited Mars took lots of pictures of its surface. These show a layer of soil that is rich in iron, which gives Mars its red colour – like rusty iron on the Earth.

Looking at Mars

There have been a number of missions to Mars.

 The **Viking** landers were two spacecraft that tested for signs of life in 1976.

 Pathfinder touched down in 1997 and released a small rover called *Sojourner*.

 Mars Express is Europe's first mission to a planet. It has been taking photos from orbit since 2004.

Mars Reconnaissance Orbiter began orbiting in 2006. It maps and takes detailed images of Mars.

 The car-sized **Curiosity** rover is the latest one to work on Mars. It landed in 2012.

How much did it cost to build, launch, and land the Mars rovers, *Spirit* and *Opportunity*?

What's happening now?

Spirit and *Opportunity* are two rovers that began exploring the Martian surface in 2004. Though *Spirit* stopped working in 2009, *Opportunity* is still operational. They have both sent back a wealth of data about the planet's surface, including evidence that huge areas of Mars were once covered by liquid water.

The NASA rover *Opportunity* holds the off-Earth roving record – by mid-2015 it completed 42.4 km (26.4 miles) on Mars.

Cameras mounted on masts give scientists all-round views of the surface.

The rover is powered by solar panels.

This image shows a 9-mm (0.35-in) hole in Mars' surface drilled and photographed by *Spirit*.

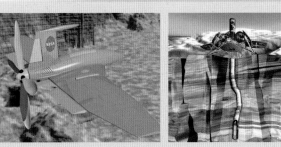

The future on Mars

Scientists are always searching for ways to unlock the secrets of the Red Planet. The suggested ideas include an aeroplane that could travel across its surface (above left) and a thermal probe that would penetrate its ice caps (above right).

In order to explore the potential of a colony in space, eight scientists lived in a self-contained dome, called Biosphere II, for two years during the early 1990s.

Living on Mars

If we do establish a base on Mars, it will have to be a self-contained structure that protects its inhabitants from both the atmosphere and the Sun's radiation. Below is an artist's impression of what a Martian base might look like.

Approximately $800 million.

Reach for the stars!

Long before the first spacecraft blasted off, people dreamed of travelling to other star systems in the hope of finding new planets. Travel between the stars is called interstellar travel, and one day it may be possible. But the difficulties are huge.

The main problem

Our fastest spaceships travel at significantly less than one thousandth of the speed of light. In terms of the vastness of space, that's incredibly slow. If we are to explore further, we need faster spacecrafts.

Space travel

A Russian physicist named Konstantin Tsiolkovsky had an idea for a spacecraft long before people went into space.

1903 model of Tsiolkovsky's futuristic spacecraft

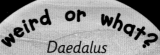
weird or what?

Daedalus wouldn't be able to stop at Barnard's Star, because slowing down would need as much fuel as speeding up. So, it would just whizz by taking pictures and measurements.

What's been done?

A long-term study into a possible interstellar spaceship took place in the 1970s. It was based on a mission to reach Barnard's Star, almost six light years away. The proposed spacecraft was named *Daedalus*.

Project *Daedalus* was planned as an unmanned space probe. It would travel at 12 per cent of the speed of light, reaching Barnard's Star within 50 years.

If interstellar travel means travel between the stars, what is intergalactic travel?

Enterprise uses warp drive to achieve faster than light (FLT) interstellar travel.

We've already been!

There have been lots of interstellar spaceships in books and films. One of the most famous is the *Star Ship Enterprise*, from *Star Trek*.

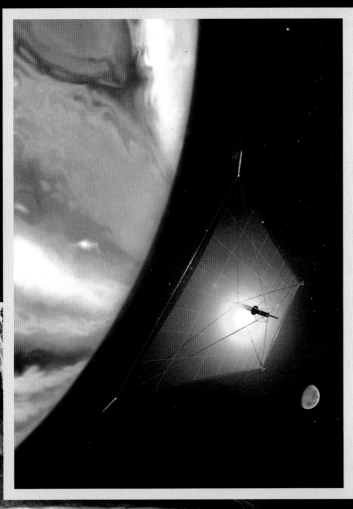

Are there other ways?

Recently, scientists have looked at using laser-powered solar sails for interstellar travel. The sail would have to be huge to collect enough energy to power the craft. It would move along because of the force of light bouncing off it. It would be helped along by powerful lasers aimed at the (mirrored) sail.

The reality

The Earth's Moon is about 1.25 light seconds away. Our fastest manned spacecraft takes three days to reach it. The fastest spacecraft built to date, *Helios 2*, would take some 19,000 years to reach our nearest star, Proxima Centauri (4.23 light years away).

The Earth is a long way from its neighbours in terms of possible space travel.

The solar system

The solar system is the name given to our immediate neighbourhood in space. It is made up of a star (the Sun), eight planets, more than 170 moons, and an assortment of comets, asteroids, and other space rocks and dust. All of these are held captive by the Sun's gravity.

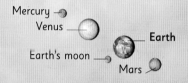

Mercury
Venus
Earth
Earth's moon
Mars

Inner planets
The asteroid belt (made up of millions of rocky bodies) circles the Sun. Mercury, Venus, Earth, and Mars are on the inner side of the belt.

What's in a name?
Most of the planets were named after Roman gods: Mercury is the winged messenger (because it appears to move swiftly); Venus is named after the goddess of love (because it is the brightest and is considered the most beautiful planet); Mars is the god of war (because of its red, blood-like colour); Jupiter is named after the king of the gods (it is the largest planet); Saturn is the father of Jupiter and the god of agriculture; Uranus is the Greek god of the sky; and Neptune is the Roman god of the sea (named after its colour).

Jupiter
Jupiter has more than 60 moons. The largest four (Ganymede, Callisto, Io, and Europa) can be seen from the Earth through binoculars.

The planets circle, or orbit, the Sun, spinning as they move.

Outer planets
The planets outside of the asteroid belt are Jupiter, Saturn, Uranus, and Neptune. Pluto used to be the most distant planet, but it failed the new planet test (opposite), and is now known as a dwarf planet.

Which planet is the smallest in our solar system?

What is a planet?

To qualify as a planet, an object has to meet these conditions.

 It must be in **orbit around a star**, just as the Earth orbits the Sun.

 It must be **large enough** for its gravity to make it round.

 Its orbit must be **cleared of other objects** (which Pluto's is not).

It must **not be a satellite** (as, for example, the Moon is a satellite of the Earth).

Saturn
Every 15 years, Saturn appears sideways to us and the rings seem to disappear.

Uranus

Neptune

Turn and learn
Eclipse of the Sun:
pp. 54-55
Venus:
pp. 58-59

Picture detective

Look through the Solar System section and see if you can identify the pictures below.

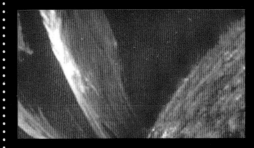

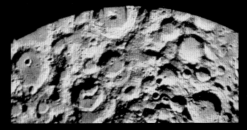

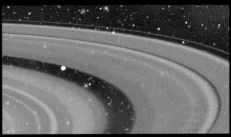

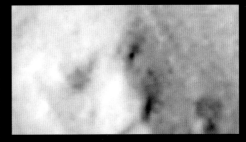

Mercury.

The Sun

The Sun's colour is best seen when reflected in water. Never look directly at the Sun.

Our Sun is a star, but it is closer to us than any other star. Like all stars, it is a massive ball of burning gas, fed by constant explosions in its core. Without it, our planet would be lifeless.

Shimmering lights can light up the skies towards the Earth's polar regions.

Solar wind

The Sun sends out a stream of invisible particles, called the solar wind. When these pass the Earth's North and South poles, they can create stunning colours.

Long lived

The Sun was born just under five billion years ago. Although it burns four million tonnes (tons) of fuel each second, it is so big that it will continue to burn for another five billion years.

Investigating the Sun

Various space probes have been designed to study the Sun.

Ulysses was launched in 1990 to look at the Sun's polar regions.

SOHO was launched in 1995 to observe the Sun and solar activity.

TRACE was launched in 1998 to study the Sun's atmosphere.

A hot spot?

White areas show places where the Sun's surface temperature is higher than elsewhere. Cooler, dark areas, called sunspots, sometimes appear on the surface.

These hotspots are called faculae.

Does the Sun spin?

The size of the Earth
compared to the Sun

A false colour image, such
as this, allows astronomers
to identify different features
on the Sun's surface.

It takes the Sun's heat about eight minutes to reach the Earth.

Solar flares

Blasts of hot gas sometimes flare up from
the Sun's surface in huge arcs or loops.
They reach thousands of kilometres
(miles) into space.

53

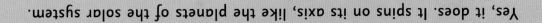

Eclipse of the Sun

It's a sunny day, but a shadow falls over the land. It is darker than a cloud covering the Sun: the light dims completely and for a few moments day turns to night. This is a solar eclipse.

The streaming light is the Sun's corona.

You are lucky if you see a total eclipse. You could wait hundreds of years to see two in the same place.

What is a solar eclipse?

A solar eclipse occurs when the Moon passes between the Sun and the Earth. By doing this, the Moon stops much of the Sun's light from reaching the Earth. The resulting shadow means that, temporarily, day turns to night in certain places.

The Sun has been covered by the Moon.

People at the centre of the Moon's shadow experience a total solar eclipse.

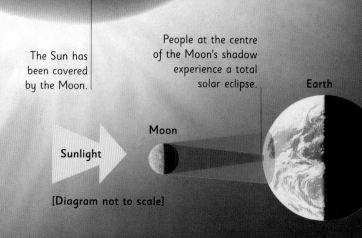

Sunlight

Moon

Earth

[Diagram not to scale]

How long would it take if you could drive to the Sun?

Stages of a solar eclipse

Time-lapse photography shows how the Moon covers the Sun in stages. In a total eclipse, the Sun is completely covered – this is called totality – for a few minutes. The Sun's outer atmosphere, the corona, can be seen clearly at this time.

There is one total solar eclipse every one to two years, and, very rarely, two in one year. The next time two solar eclipses occur in the same year will be in 2057.

It takes about one hour for the Moon to block the Sun's light, once it begins to move across the Sun.

Ringed wonder

In the instant before the Sun disappears behind the Moon, sunlight sometimes streams between mountains on the Moon's surface, producing a stunning effect known as a diamond-ring.

The diamond-ring effect lasts for just a few seconds.

The map shows the paths of total solar eclipses from 2012 to 2021.

Plotting eclipses

Total solar eclipses occur once every 15 months or so, and maps such as these are used to plot the path of future eclipses. The shadow from a total eclipse follows a narrow path and often falls on an ocean – so it won't be seen (unless you're on a boat!).

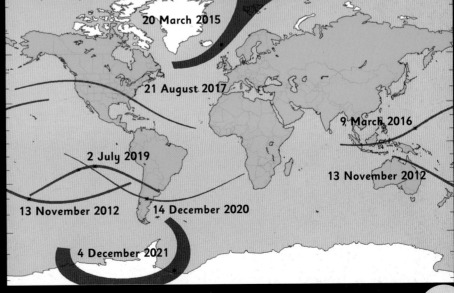

20 March 2015

21 August 2017

9 March 2016

2 July 2019

13 November 2012

13 November 2012

14 December 2020

4 December 2021

If you travelled at a speed of 150 kph (93 mph), it would take you 114 years.

Mercury

The closest planet to the Sun, and far smaller than the Earth, Mercury has blistering hot days, but freezing nights. The nights get cold because Mercury has no atmosphere to trap the Sun's heat.

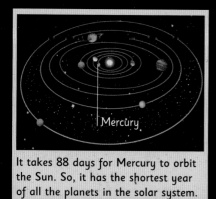

Mercury

It takes 88 days for Mercury to orbit the Sun. So, it has the shortest year of all the planets in the solar system.

Surface mapping

In 1974 and 1975, the space probe *Mariner 10* flew within 327 km (203 miles) of Mercury's surface. It took hundreds of photographs, covering just under half the planet.

An easy target

Mariner 10 provided close-ups of Mercury that showed a heavily scarred surface. Rather like the Earth's moon, this planet was battered by asteroids long ago. It is covered with bowl-shaped hollows, called craters, where the asteroids hit. The surface has hardly changed in the last billion years.

weird or what?

One of Mercury's craters (the Caloris Basin) is so large that the British Isles could fit comfortably into it.

Many of Mercury's craters are named after famous painters, authors, and musicians, such as Mozart, Beethoven, Michelangelo, and Bach.

In Roman mythology, who was Mercury?

Red hot

As Mercury faces the Sun, temperatures reach a sizzling 427°C (800°F), hot enough to melt lead. Mercury is the second-hottest planet, after Venus.

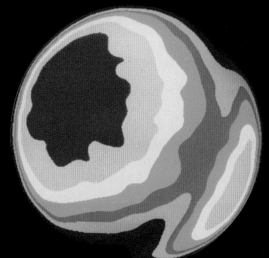

This is a temperature map of Mercury – red shows where the most heat is found.

This false colour picture of planet Mercury, taken by *MESSENGER*, is used to show the geological features of the planet.

A small planet

Mercury is the smallest planet in the solar system. Pluto, which is smaller, has been reclassified as a dwarf planet.

Cross-section of Mercury, showing its iron core.

Long journey

Launched in 2004, space probe *MESSENGER* set out on a journey to Mercury. It reached the planet in 2008, flew by three times, and then entered Mercury's orbit in 2011. By 2013, it had mapped its entire surface.

57

From the Earth, Venus is easiest to see when it appears to be farthest in the sky from the Sun.

The morning star

You wouldn't want to visit Venus. You'd be crushed in an instant and your remains fried to a crisp. This barren planet is covered in acid clouds, and it has an incredibly dense atmosphere.

Where is it?

Venus is the brightest planet. It can be seen in the early morning or early evening sky, depending on where it is in its orbit around the Sun. That's why it's known as the morning or evening star.

A mass of clouds

The cloud layer is too thick to let much sunlight penetrate, but it does reflect a lot of light. In fact, after the Moon, Venus is the brightest object in our night sky.

Caused by chemicals in the atmosphere, the dark cloud tops (shown exaggerated in this image) blow around the planet.

Venus's rocky plains without cloud cover

Which planet is the nearest in size to the Earth?

So what is it like?

This false colour picture of Venus was made from data collected by probes, including the *Magellan* probe, sent to Venus between 1989 and 1992. The blue areas represent huge plains of solid lava. The white, green, and brown areas are higher land, such as hills, mountains, volcanoes, and valleys.

The surface temperature is about 482°C (900°F).

Turn and learn

The red planet:
pp. 64–65
The ringed planet:
pp. 70–71

Venus spins on its axis slower than any other planet. It takes 243 Earth days to just spin once.

Surface of Venus

Maat Mons is the highest volcano on Venus. This view of the surface of the planet exaggerates the height of Maat Mons to show its slopes in more detail. The volcano is named after Ma'at, the Egyptian goddess of truth and justice.

Venus spins in the opposite direction to the Earth, meaning the Sun rises in the west and sets in the east.

Venus. Its diameter is just 650 km (400 miles) smaller than the Earth's.

Third rock from the Sun

Our home planet, the Earth, is the only one in the solar system capable of supporting life as we know it. It's the right temperature because it's neither too close to the Sun, nor too far from it.

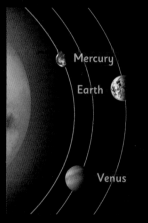

Mercury

Earth

Venus

The Earth is the third planet from the Sun. It takes 365.25 days to orbit the Sun.

Take a deep breath

The Earth is surrounded by an atmosphere made up of gases – mostly nitrogen and oxygen, with traces of carbon dioxide and other gases mixed in.

On this globe, the ocean's warm areas are coloured red, and its cooler areas are blue.

A warm blanket

The Earth's atmosphere and oceans play a crucial role in keeping its temperature stable. They absorb the Sun's heat and move it around the planet. This helps keep the temperature suitable for life.

Which two planets lie between the Earth and the Sun?

Cut open an onion, and you'll see that it's composed of layers. The Earth has layers too, and they get hotter and hotter the deeper they go.

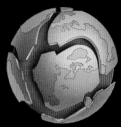

A moving crust

The Earth's surface layer, or crust, is a shell of solid rock. This crust is broken up into plates, which shift around constantly on a middle layer of molten, or liquid, rock. The Earth's core is solid.

The Earth's plates

The Earth is constantly spinning. It takes 24 hours to turn completely on its axis.

Danger zones

The areas where the Earth's plates move against each other are often weak spots where volcanoes and earthquakes are common.

Molten lava erupts from a volcano in Hawaii, which is located where there is a weak place in the Earth's crust.

Turn and learn

The Earth's atmosphere:
pp. 6-7

The Earth is surrounded by a thin halo – our precious atmosphere.

The Earth is the only planet in our solar system with an atmosphere in which animals and plants (as we know them) can breathe.

The Moon

The Earth has one natural satellite – the Moon. It is the brightest object in the night sky (although it doesn't produce its own light). It is a bleak place, with no water, no plants, no air, and no life.

Stretched flat, the Moon's surface would almost cover North and South America.

Spinning around and around

It takes 27 days for the Moon to travel around, or orbit, the Earth. As it travels, it spins slowly. It actually spins just once during each orbit of the Earth.

The Moon's orbit

From the Earth, we only see the nearside of the Moon.

Earth

The farside of the Moon is never seen from the Earth.

Only one side of the Moon is...

The Moon may have been formed after an immense collision that sent debris into orbit around the Earth.

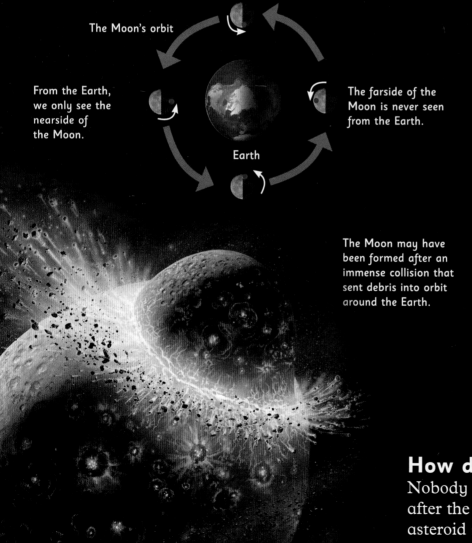

How did it form?

Nobody really knows, but it was possibly after the Earth was hit by a Mars-sized asteroid some 4.5 billion years ago.

How does the Moon appear so bright, if it doesn't produce any light?

The Sun alters the tides, too.

The Moon's gravitational pull gives the Earth's oceans a bulge. Sea levels change in particular areas as the Earth spins.

The red arrow represents the Earth's rotational spin.

The Moon

... ever seen from the Earth.

Tide control

The rise and fall of the Earth's oceans twice daily is mainly caused by the Moon's gravitational pull, which makes the ocean bulge a few metres in one direction. This bulge moves very slowly, but appears to sweep round the Earth as it turns.

Away from the bulge, it's low tide.

As a place passes through the bulge, it's high tide.

A battered past

The Moon has been badly battered by asteroids in its long history, leaving its surface full of craters.

Moon missions

Many unmanned space probes have been sent to investigate the Moon, including those below.

Luna 3, a Soviet probe, took the first pictures of the far side of the Moon in 1959.

Luna 9, a Soviet probe, made the first soft landing on the Moon in 1966.

Lunar Prospector, a US probe, discovered ice near the Moon's poles in 1999.

Lunar Reconnaissance Orbiter, a NASA probe, has been mapping the Moon since 2009.

It reflects the Sun's light.

The Red Planet

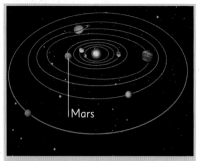

Mars is the fourth planet from the Sun. It has an atmosphere, seasons, huge mountains, and icy poles.

Mars was named by the Romans after their god of war, because its red colour reminded them of blood. That's why it is also known as the Red Planet.

Earth

Mars

A Martian day – called a "sol" – lasts a little over 24 hours...

An alternate Earth?

Mars is half the size of the Earth, and conditions are very different to those on our planet. Although Mars has a thin atmosphere and seasons, nothing grows there. Its red, desert-like surface is littered with dust and rocks.

I spy two moons

Mars has two lumpy moons that were discovered in 1877. They are so tiny that astronomers think they were asteroids pulled into orbit around Mars by its gravity.

Phobos

Deimos

Deimos (which means "terror" in Greek) is 16 km by 12 km (10 miles by 7 miles).

Phobos (which means "fear" in Greek) measures 28 km by 20 km (17 miles by 12 miles).

Is the Martian sky blue, like ours?

Is there water?

Mars is such a cold planet that its water is mostly in the form of ice. However, dried up water channels and lakes tell us huge amounts of liquid water flowed over Mars in the past. Downhill streaks seen in 2015 were formed by very recent water flows.

Dried water channel

… (24 Earth hours, 39 minutes, and a few seconds).

A face on Mars

In 1976, *Viking 1 Orbiter* sent a series of shots that showed a "face" on the planet's surface. Many saw this as an enormous sculpture built by intelligent life. It's actually a mountain.

Recent picture of the "face".

The first blurry picture of the "face".

That's definitely Martian!

There are a number of notable features on the surface of Mars.

The planet experiences strong winds that create immense **dust storms**.

Mars has two **polar ice caps** – one at its south pole and one at its north pole.

The **Olympus Mons volcano** is the largest in the solar system.

The **Valles Marineris canyon** would stretch across the USA.

No. If you stood on Mars, you would see a pink sky.

King of the planets

Jupiter, the solar system's largest planet, is a gas giant made up mainly of hydrogen. It is huge. If all the planets in the solar system were combined, Jupiter would still weigh more than twice as much.

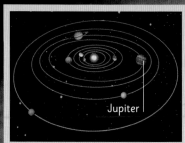

Jupiter is the fifth planet from the Sun. More than 1,300 Earth-sized planets could fit into Jupiter.

A thick cloud cover

Jupiter's cloudy atmosphere is about 1,000 km (600 miles) deep, but the clouds do not hide a solid crust. They swirl over an inner liquid layer of hydrogen and helium.

Jupiter's bands are caused by the movements and mixing of different gases in the atmosphere as the planet spins.

The Great Red Spot reaches about 8 km (5 miles) above the surrounding clouds. Within it, winds reach a speed of 400 kph (250 mph).

The shrinking storm

The Great Red Spot is a storm that is almost the size of the Earth. Observed since 1666, its swirling mass takes about a week to turn anti-clockwise. Scientists have observed that the spot, which could once fit three Earths, is rapidly shrinking.

Can you think why the *Galileo* spacecraft was so named?

Jupiter takes 12 Earth years to orbit the Sun.

As seen from space, the Earth's colour scheme comes from its land, oceans, and white clouds. Jupiter is painted in oranges by the clouds of chemicals in its atmosphere.

In a spin
Despite its size, Jupiter spins faster than any other planet. In fact, one rotation takes just under 10 hours. It spins so fast that it bulges slightly at the equator, and its clouds are pulled into thick bands.

Let's take a closer look
The *Galileo* spacecraft reached Jupiter in 1995 and began to orbit the planet. It also dropped a probe into Jupiter's atmosphere. Before being destroyed after just 58 minutes in the intense heat and pressure, the probe sent back information about the planet.

weird or what?
Jupiter is shrinking slightly each year because it is being squeezed by its gravity. The energy produced means it creates more heat than it gets from the Sun.

Galileo ended its long mission when it dropped into Jupiter and was destroyed in 2003.

This is Io, one of Jupiter's many moons orbiting the planet.

The probe entered Jupiter's atmosphere at 170,000 kph (106,000 mph). Its descent was slowed by a 2.5-m- (8-ft-) wide parachute.

The *Galileo* probe was about the size and weight of a fairly small cow.

No stopping me now!
Galileo finished its main mission in 1997, but incredibly, it survived until 2003, sending back lots of extra information about Jupiter and its moons. You can discover more about Jupiter's moons on pages 68 and 69.

Jupiter's moons

Jupiter has 67 known moons (and probably many more that haven't yet been spotted). Most are tiny, and dark in colour. Scientists think many of them are asteroids that have been caught by Jupiter's immense gravity.

Ganymede (right), the solar system's largest moon, makes our moon (left) seem rather small.

Europa

The Galilean moons

Jupiter's largest moons are Io, Europa, Ganymede, and Callisto. One of these – Io – was shown by *Voyager 1* to have volcanoes that are so active that its surface is constantly disturbed.

There are rings, too

Jupiter also has a ring system, which was first seen in images captured by the *Voyager 1* space probe in 1979. The rings were formed by dust kicked up when meteorites hit Jupiter's four inner moons.

Moon spotting

The four largest moons were named by a German astronomer, Simon Marius. They were studied by Galileo Galilei in 1610 (who thought at first that they were small stars). They can be seen from Earth with good binoculars.

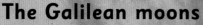

Simon Marius

Io

Turn and learn

Jupiter:
pp. 66-67
Our Moon:
pp. 62-63

Who is credited with discovering Jupiter's largest moons?

Diameter: 3,130 km (1,945 miles)

False colour image of Europa

Europa is not striped with red! False colour images, such as this one of Europa's lines, are helpful as they show features very clearly.

Europa has an icy surface criss-crossed with lines that suggest deeper activity. Scientists believe the ice covers a layer of liquid salty water – a huge ocean, with a possibility of aquatic life. In fact, it has become the most likely place for extraterrestrial life in our solar system.

Diameter: 5,268 km (3,273 miles)

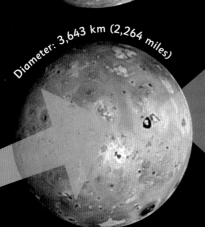

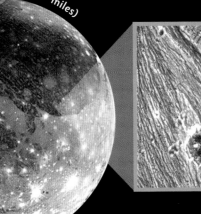

Ganymede is the largest known moon in our solar system.

Ganymede is larger than Mercury, but is not a planet because it doesn't orbit the Sun. Scientists think this moon has a molten core, surrounded by a rocky mantle, possible salt water, and an ice shell.

Diameter: 3,643 km (2,264 miles)

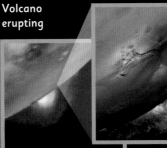
Volcano erupting

Material is thrown a long way into space by Io's volcanoes.

Io is constantly undergoing volcanic eruptions across its surface, resulting in its amazing yellow-orange colour. In fact, it has more than 100 active volcanoes! The eruptions happen because this moon is continually tugged and pushed around by the gravities of Jupiter and the other three moons.

Diameter: 4,806 km (2,986 miles)

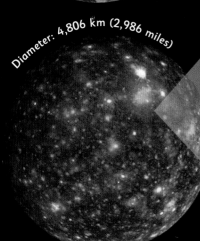

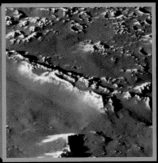

Callisto is incredibly battered, the result of thousands of meteorite strikes.

Callisto's dark, dirty, and icy crust is covered with craters. The largest, Valhalla, has shockwaves that spread out some 3,000 km (1,865 miles). Astronomers believe the crust hides a rocky core.

Saturn

Saturn is the second-largest planet in our solar system. It is huge. You could line up nine Earths in a row across Saturn, but as it is largely composed of gas, you couldn't land a craft on its surface.

Saturn is the sixth planet from the Sun in the solar system.

A ringed beauty

Saturn isn't the only planet with rings, but it is the only planet whose rings are easily visible to us because of their large area. The rings are made up of ice, dust, and rock.

Ice in Saturn's rings reflects light. That's why we see them so well.

Saturn spins around once every 10 hours 39 minutes, making it bulge at the middle as it spins.

Saturn is named after...

Blown away

Even if you could land on Saturn, you'd be blown away pretty quickly by the incredibly strong winds. Winds around the planet's equator can reach 1,800 km (1,100 miles) an hour.

High winds on the Earth would be very light winds on Saturn.

70

Turn and learn

Cassini-Huygens:
p. 25
Planet names:
p. 50

Each of Saturn's rings have a thickness of about 1 km (0.6 mile) or less. The seven main rings are made up of about 10,000 ringlets. They extend around 282,000 km (175,000 miles).

... the Roman god of agriculture.

A mission to Saturn

In 1997, the *Cassini* spacecraft blasted off for Saturn with a spaceprobe named *Huygens* on board. *Cassini* went into orbit around Saturn in June 2004 and *Huygens* was dropped onto its largest moon, Titan, in January 2005.

Vital statistics

Cassini sends back lots of information because of some of its amazing features.

Titan is difficult to study because of its thick orange clouds.

Huygens

The craft contains more than 12 km (7.5 miles) of **wires**.

It is the **size of a coach**, but is only a little heavier in weight than an elephant.

More than half its weight is made up by its **fuel**.

It carries a **camera** that could spot a coin from almost 4 km (2.5 miles).

Huygens is now the furthest human-made object ever to land on a celestial body.

On the job!

Huygens took a little less than two and a half hours to descend to the surface of Titan, and then worked there for around an hour. It transmitted data for that entire duration, and remained active for far longer than anyone had hoped.

Jupiter, Neptune, and Uranus all have rings.

Distant twins

Uranus and Neptune are the seventh and eighth planets from the Sun, and are often referred to as twins because of their similar size and make-up.

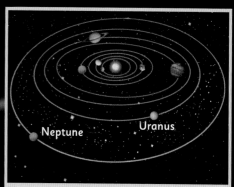

Uranus and Neptune have atmospheres of hydrogen and helium gas, with traces of poisonous methane gas. Below this, the planets are covered in ice and slush.

Uranus

Uranus was discovered in 1781 by William Herschel. He named it *Georgium Sidus*, or George's Star, in honour of King George III of Great Britain. This name was not popular, so it was later renamed Uranus.

Colours

Uranus looks a lot plainer than this false colour suggests, but this image gives astronomers a lot of information about the planet.

Uranus is encircled by 12 narrow rings made of rocks and dust.

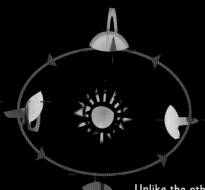

Unlike the other planets, Uranus orbits the Sun on its side.

Unusual seasons

It takes 84 Earth years for Uranus to orbit the Sun. The poles each experience 42 years of "winter", then 42 years of "summer". For 21 of those years, they are each in continual darkness or light.

This close-up picture shows Uranus's rings.

In Greek mythology, who was Uranus?

Neptune

A blue planet, Neptune is named after the ancient Roman god of the sea. Neptune takes 165 Earth years to orbit the Sun. So, since its discovery in 1846, it has only completed one full orbit.

Neptune's moons

Neptune has 14 known moons. Its largest moon, Triton, is bitterly cold and has a heavily pitted surface as well as active volcano-like eruptions.

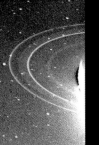

These two pictures show the rings of Neptune. The planet has at least four faint rings made up of dust particles.

Neptune is a very cold planet. This isn't surprising as it is 30 times farther away from the Sun than the Earth. From Neptune, the Sun probably looks like a very, very bright star.

A day on Neptune lasts 16 hours 7 minutes.

Big storm

Neptune is incredibly stormy. In 1989, *Voyager 2* discovered a storm the size of the Earth on Neptune's surface. The storm lasted several years.

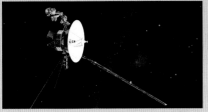

Miranda (one of Uranus's moons)

Pictures from space

Voyager 2 has flown past both Uranus (in 1986) and Neptune (in 1989). It discovered ten of Uranus's moons and six of Neptune's. Most information had to be gathered in just a few hours as it sped on its way.

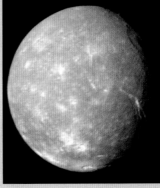
Titania (one of Uranus's moons)

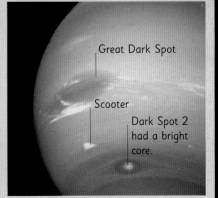
Great Dark Spot

Scooter

Dark Spot 2 had a bright core.

This picture of Neptune, taken by *Voyager 2* in 1989, shows two dark storms (the Dark Spots) and the fast-moving cloud Scooter. Both of the Dark Spots have now disappeared.

Pluto

Pluto, a ball of ice and rock, was discovered in 1930, and became our solar system's ninth planet. However, in 2006 it was reclassified as a dwarf planet.

Why isn't it a planet?

Pluto was reclassified as it is just one of many objects in what is known as the Kuiper Belt. Two of the other named dwarf planets in our solar system are Ceres and Eris.

The Kuiper Belt is a band of comet-like objects that orbit the Sun beyond Neptune.

A frozen world

At times, the surface of Pluto has an atmosphere. It appears when Pluto is closer to the Sun and its ice is warmed to release gas, but it refreezes and disappears when Pluto moves farther away from the Sun.

So how big is Pluto?

Pluto is estimated to be about 2,370 km (1,473 miles) across, and Eris is a similar size. Even some of the solar system's moons are larger than Pluto, including our moon!

Pluto	Moon	Earth
2,370 km	3,400 km	12,750 km
(1,473 miles)	(2,100 miles)	(8,000 miles)

Eris   Pluto   Ceres

Can you guess how long it takes the Sun's light to reach Pluto?

Pluto's orbit

Pluto orbits the Sun slightly differently to the main planets. Its orbit also takes it nearer to the Sun than Neptune for part of the 248 Earth years of its orbit.

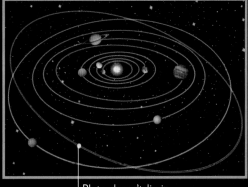

Pluto doesn't lie in the same plane as the eight planets of the solar system.

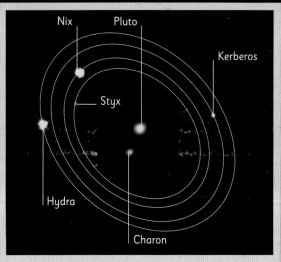

Pluto has five known moons. The largest is called Charon. It moves around Pluto every six days. Two smaller moons, Nix and Hydra, were discovered in 2005. Kerberos and Styx were discovered in 2011 and 2012, respectively.

Pluto takes 248 Earth years to orbit the Sun. Its surface is thought to be mainly frozen nitrogen, with traces of methane.

New Horizons is one of the fastest spacecraft ever to be launched.

New Horizons blasted into space on board an *Atlas 5* rocket.

Dwarf planets

Just look at this picture comparing the size of Pluto with other dwarf planets. Eris was only discovered in 2005. Ceres is the size of the US state Texas. It lies in the main asteroid belt between Mars and Jupiter, and is the biggest celestial body there.

A mission to Pluto

In 2006, the US space agency NASA launched a spacecraft called *New Horizons* to study Pluto and other objects in the Kuiper Belt. In 2015, it flew by Pluto and is now headed for an encounter with a Kuiper Belt object in 2019.

Comets and meteors

In between the planets, space contains gas, dust, icy comets, and rocks called asteroids. Comets, which can be thought of as space snowballs, vary in size. When one moves close to the Sun, the Sun's heat turns its ice to gas, and dust is released. The gas and dust form a huge head (coma), and two tails – one of gas, the other of dust. If the head and tails are bright enough, they can be seen from the Earth.

Collision course

In 1994, a ball of fire the size of a small planet exploded on Jupiter. It happened when the first of more than 20 fragments of a comet ploughed into the planet.

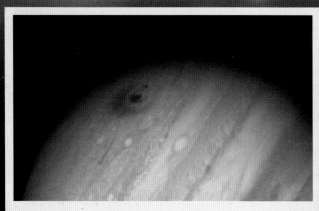

Crash landing

When comet Shoemaker-Levy 9 collided with Jupiter, it was the biggest collision of two solar system bodies observed by humankind.

Comet Shoemaker-Levy 9 sent fireballs more than 3,000 km (1,900 miles) above the clouds of Jupiter.

How often are there meteor showers?

For six days, fragments of comet hit Jupiter.

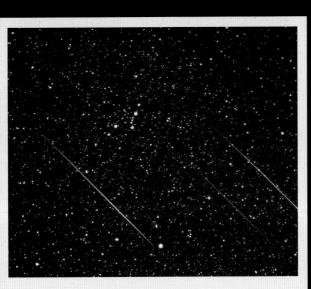

Meteor shower
When pieces of comet burn up in the Earth's atmosphere, they produce meteor showers – bright shooting stars that race across the night sky, as in this picture of Leonid meteors.

Picture detective
Look through the Comets and Meteors section and see if you can identify the pictures below.

Spot the difference
Here's a guide to space objects you'll find in this section.

Meteors, or "shooting stars", are short-lived streaks of light produced by space dust speeding through the Earth's atmosphere.

Asteroids are basically giant boulders of rock, some so big that they have their own tiny moons.

Meteorites are bits of space rock that survive the journey through the Earth's atmosphere and hit the Earth.

Comets are space snowballs, made from dust and ice, that orbit the Sun.

Space junk is made of man-made things that have been left or lost in space.

Turn and learn
Asteroids:
pp. 82-83
Space debris:
pp. 86-87

Many times a year. Most reoccur at the same time each year.

Just passing

Comets are huge, dirty space snowballs. Made of ice, rock, and dust, they hurtle through space on huge orbits around the Sun to the outer edge of our solar system.

Comets can reach tens of kilometres (miles) across.

A comet from Earth
In early 2007, the brightest comet for 40 years, comet McNaught, hit the skies. It was so bright that it could be seen during the night as well as during the day.

Distant visitor
The closest that comet Hyakutake came to the Earth was 15 million km (9.3 million miles). It was spotted in 1996 by a man in Japan who was looking through binoculars.

A comet's tail...

Halley's comet
Comets often reappear at regular intervals as they travel past the Earth. One of the most famous, Halley's comet, returns every 75 or 76 years. It is named after astronomer Edmond Halley who predicted it would return in 1758, after being sighted four times before.

Edmond Halley, 1656–1742

Halley's comet travels up to 240,000 kph (150,000 mph).

Where did the word "comet" come from?

... can trail for millions of kilometres (miles).

Tail light

If a comet's orbit takes it close to the Sun, its surface begins to evaporate, releasing gas and dust. This results in two spectacular tails that point away from the Sun.

Tail piece

The yellow or white tail is made up of dust. The longer and thinner blue tail is made up of gas. Sometimes the two show up as one tail.

Tall tail

These pictures show how the comet's tail changes as it moves towards, and then away from, the Sun.

Halley's comet in 1910

From the Greek word *komêtês*, which means "long-haired".

Shooting stars

A flash of light briefly streaks across the sky, and then disappears. It is probably a meteor – a common sight. Meteors are also known as shooting stars.

Fragments of Canon Diablo meteorite from the Barringer Crater in Arizona, USA.

What is it?

A meteor is a short-lived streak of light produced by a piece of space dust – a meteoroid – burning up as it speeds through the Earth's atmosphere. This happens about 90 km (56 miles) above the ground. A piece of space rock that survives the journey and lands on the Earth is called a meteorite.

Sparkling showers

When several fragments of a former comet or asteroid enter the Earth's atmosphere and burn up, it can result in spectacular showers. One famous shower takes place every November, when the Earth passes through a swarm of meteoroids known as the Leonids.

Bomb blast

When the Wolf Creek meteorite crater was formed 1–2 million years ago it exploded like an atomic bomb. Nearly a perfect circle, the crater is 853 m (2,798 ft) in diameter.

Wolf Creek Crater
Great Sandy Desert, Western Australia

How many meteorites land on the Earth each year?

Powerful meteorites

There have been a number of spectacular meteorite strikes on our planet.

A meteorite strike in **Tunguska, Siberia** destroyed miles of forest in 1908.

The **Barringer Crater** in Arizona was formed 50,000 years ago. It is 1,609 m (5,278 ft) across.

Many believe the **dinosaurs** were wiped out by a meteorite strike 65 million years ago.

Fire from the sky

People have feared meteorites for centuries. Some saw them as fiery dragons, others as weapons sent by angry gods.

hands on

See the impact of meteorites by dropping different size balls onto a tray of damp sand. This shows what happens when a meteorite hits a planet's surface – it leaves a crater.

A meteoroid strikes our atmosphere at up to 72 km per second (160,000 mph).

I like you!

Most meteorites will attract a magnet, because of their iron content.

A lone meteor

A meteor that isn't part of a shower is called a sporadic meteor. Incredibly bright meteors are called fireballs.

About 3,000 meteorites, weighing more than 1 kg (2 lb) each, land every year.

The asteroid belt

Asteroids are chunks of rock. Some are small enough to hold in your hand, while others are larger than a mountain. Most asteroids in our solar system orbit the Sun within the asteroid belt, which lies between Jupiter and Mars.

Leftovers
Scientists believe that asteroids are the bits and pieces left over after the formation of the solar system.

Asteroids can be pulled in by the gravity of nearby planets to become moons.

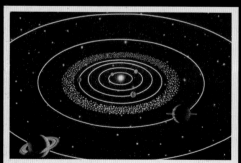

Most asteroids exist in the asteroid belt, of which about 400,000 have been identified. It takes between three and six years for asteroids to orbit the Sun.

Hurry across!
Despite the existence of millions of asteroids in the belt, spacecraft such as Galileo (right), have crossed this area of space without colliding with a single one. That's because most of the asteroids are thousands of kilometres (miles) apart.

Why aren't most asteroids spherical, like the planets?

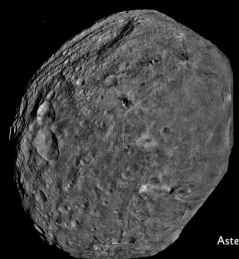

A real whopper

The brightest and second largest asteroid in the belt is Vesta. It has a diameter of 530 km (329 miles). Ceres is the largest and the first asteroid to be discovered. It is now also classed as a dwarf planet.

Asteroid Vesta

Vast in size

The asteroid belt contains millions of asteroids. Scientists estimate there are around two million with a diameter larger than 1 km (0.6 miles), and 200 larger than 100 km (60 miles).

Chicxulub Crater in Mexico

Collision course

Stray asteroids or comets occasionally collide with planets, creating huge craters. An asteroid may have crashed into the Earth 65 million years ago, causing a catastrophic climate change that wiped out the dinosaurs.

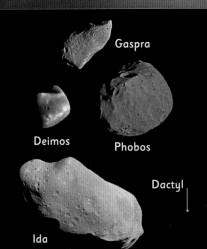

Gaspra

Deimos

Phobos

Dactyl

Asteroids range in size and shape. Only the largest tend to be round.

Ida

Just passing

The Galileo spacecraft took the first clear photographs of the asteroid Gaspra, when it passed through the belt en route to Jupiter in 1991. It later took a picture of Ida, which is 55 km (35 miles) long, when it passed through the asteroid belt again in 1993. The shot included Ida's moon, Dactyl – the first evidence that asteroids can have satellites of their own.

Because they are too small. They lack the gravity to pull themselves into a ball shape.

Asteroid landing

Near-Earth asteroids are asteroids that pass relatively close to the Earth. This means they are the easiest asteroids for scientists to study. In fact, two spacecraft have successfully landed on them.

The launch of NEAR spacecraft in 1996.

Asteroid Itokawa

One asteroid that has been studied is Itokawa, which is tiny. A Japanese spacecraft, *Hayabusa*, was sent to collect dust samples from Itokawa, and returned these to the Earth in June 2010.

Hayabusa (which means "falcon" in Japanese) took this picture of the asteroid Itokawa, which was named after a Japanese rocket scientist.

Touchdown

Hayabusa landed on Itokawa on 20 November 2005, and remained on the surface for just 30 minutes. It landed again briefly on the 25th. Nobody was sure whether or not it picked up samples, until it arrived back on the Earth in 2010.

Asteroid Eros

Eros is about 33 km (20 miles) in length. The spaceprobe *NEAR-Shoemaker*'s mission was to orbit Eros. NEAR stands for Near Earth Asteroid Rendezvous.

Hayabusa carried a miniature lander, but this was unsuccessful.

The spacecraft's box-shaped body is just over 1 m (3 ft) in height.

Eros is named after a Greek god. Can you guess which one?

NEAR-Shoemaker

At the end of its mission, in February 2001, the team decided to try landing the probe on Eros to show that it could be done. As it neared the asteroid for landing it sent a series of 69 increasingly detailed shots of the surface.

February 2000
Eros picture made up from six images pieced together

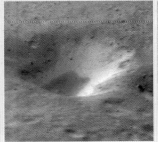

January 2001
Taken from 38 km (24 miles) above Eros, showing a crater

February 2001
Eros' surface taken from a distance of 700 m (2,300 ft)

What did the probe find?

Some asteroids are basically loose piles of rubble, moving together in space. Scientists discovered Eros to be solid. Like many other asteroids, it is perhaps as old as the Earth.

A close approach

NEAR-Shoemaker spent a year orbiting Eros, during which time it sent back lots of useful information to the Earth about the asteroid.

It takes Eros just over five hours to rotate on its axis.

Researchers have said that a person who could jump 1 m (3 ft) on the Earth, would be able to jump 1.6 km (1 mile) on Eros because of its weak gravity.

Eros was the Greek god of love.

Space debris

An astronaut works on a spacecraft, and loses a tool. An ageing satellite begins to break up. A panel is knocked off a space station... space is littered with junk, and the problem is getting worse.

Cosmic litter

Examples of unexpected space rubbish include the following.

 A **glove**, lost by an American astronaut on a spacewalk in 1965.

 Rubbish bags, released by the *Mir* space station.

 Two cameras, reported lost in space by astronauts.

 Nuts and **bolts**, lost when satellites were being repaired.

Tracking the junk

An incredible amount of junk is orbiting the Earth. The path of anything larger than a tennis ball is tracked by scientists – currently more than 20,000 objects are being watched. Experts believe that, in total, well over half a million objects larger than 1 cm ($^1/_2$ in) are orbiting our planet.

At what height does space litter orbit the Earth?

Falling to Earth

Debris falls to Earth regularly, but there is only one report of someone being struck by metal from space. After all, most of the Earth is ocean.

What are the dangers?

Items of junk are generally far apart in space, but problems arise when a fast-moving object, moving at speeds of up to 28,200 kph (17,500 mph), slams into a spacecraft or space station. This crater in a window surface on the space shuttle *Challenger* is typical of the damage caused.

Bits of space debris eventually fall into the Earth's atmosphere, where they either burn up or crash to the ground. This is the main propellant tank of the second stage of a *Delta 2* launch vehicle. It weighs approximately 250 kg (551 lb).

What can be done?

Before every launch, mission controllers make sure their spacecraft will not travel near any dangerous junk. Scientists are hoping to find a way to clear the Earth's orbit, but a solution is a long way off. These suggestions are being considered – lasers that can break objects up; space-rubbish ships; and technology that can tug rubbish lower so it burns up in the atmosphere.

Mission controllers keep a close watch on the path of their space launches.

87

Mysteries of space

Black holes, alien life, the Big Bang... space and its mysteries have always fascinated people, and inspired artists and writers. We know quite a lot about space, but there is far more we don't know. So what is fact, and what is fantasy?

Lives of the stars

Mysteries, such as how stars are born in nebulae and die in supernovae, are gradually being solved with the help of incredibly powerful telescopes. But there is a long way to go.

Supernova remnant
Cassiopeia A

Which novel about an alien invasion from Mars was published in 1898?

Illustration from a 1950s sci-fi comic

Fact or fiction?

Curiosity about aliens has produced lots of ideas about what they might look like. In some books and films, aliens look much like humans, with two arms and legs, or resemble giant blobs or spiders.

Stormtrooper from *Star Wars*™

Space monster toy

Flying saucers

Lots of people claim to have seen flying saucers, or Unidentified Flying Objects (UFOs), while some claim to have visited alien spaceships. But do UFOs really exist? What is this image? Turn to page 90 to find out more.

Picture detective

Look through the Mysteries of Space pages and try to identify the pictures below.

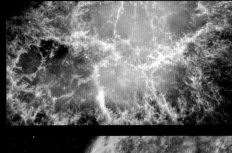

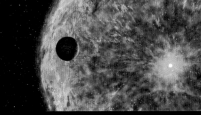

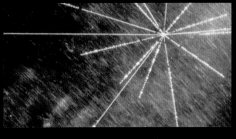

Turn and learn

Aliens:
pp. 92-93
Life on Mars:
pp. 94-95

The War of the Worlds by H. G. Wells.

UFOs

Flying saucer-shaped objects, crop circles, lights in the night sky… people have long claimed to see and find evidence of UFOs (Unidentified Flying Objects). Look at some of the claims yourself. What do you think?

Crop circles

These are intricate designs made from flattened areas of corn. Some believe they are the landing sites of flying saucers, but many have been proved to have been made by humans.

Was it a strange craft?

The Apollo picture shown on the previous page was thoroughly investigated, and found to be nothing more mysterious than the floodlight boom, used when astronauts left the spacecraft.

Is it a UFO coming in to land…

The idea that intelligent life exists outside our solar system has always seemed to intrigue people. This cave painting is thousands of years old. It appears to depict an extraterrestrial encounter.

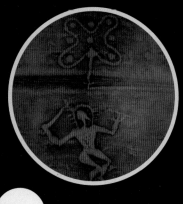

Which country do you think has the most reported incidents of UFOs?

Artists have often drawn space ships as oval metal discs.

In the news
Some newspapers have even reported the landing of alien spacecraft. The most famous of these incidents occurred at a place called Roswell, USA, when strange debris was found in 1947.

Waiting for an answer
This famous image, below, has still not been explained, although some suggest it may be the mirror from a truck. It was taken by a farmer in Oregon in 1950.

Is this a truck's wing mirror, or something more mysterious?

... or not?

What was Roswell?
People claimed the debris found at Roswell was of a spacecraft that crashed. Early newspaper reports called it a "flying disc". However, the military said it was a top secret weather balloon.

Crash debris is investigated at Roswell in the 1940s.

An alien spacecraft?
Roswell resulted in a number of books, films, stories, and general speculation. However, most people now believe that it was a weather balloon.

An Air Force Weather Balloon in 1995, eight years after Roswell

Road sign in Roswell, USA – the scene of spaceship investigations in the 1940s.

The USA.

91

Is anyone there?

If there are aliens, it is unlikely they will speak the same languages as those spoken on Earth, so communication may be a problem. Coded signals have been sent into space. People are also listening for signals from space.

SETI

The Search for Extraterrestrial Intelligence (SETI) uses powerful radio telescopes to scan for alien signals. However, so far nothing has been found.

Arecibo radio telescope, Puerto Rico

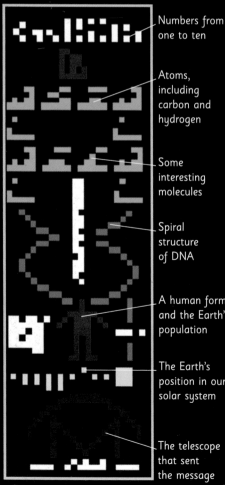

Numbers from one to ten

Atoms, including carbon and hydrogen

Some interesting molecules

Spiral structure of DNA

A human form and the Earth's population

The Earth's position in our solar system

The telescope that sent the message

Message into space

In 1974, astronomers at Arecibo, Puerto Rico, sent a radio message from us to the stars. It was sent towards a cluster of stars called M13, where it will arrive in 25,000 years. We may then get a reply after another 25,000 years (if anybody is there to read it!).

This is the Parkes radio telescope in Canberra, Australia. It was used by the SETI institute from the 1990s to the early 2000s.

The Arecibo message lasts three minutes. It consists of 1,679 pulses, which when arranged form a pictogram (see left). The pictogram explains the basis of life.

Who founded the SETI institute?

A plaque into space

The spaceprobes *Pioneer 10* and *11* carry engraved metal plaques. It is a space equivalent of a message in a bottle! The plaques reveal the Earth's place in the solar system, the probes' route away from the Earth, and give the outlines of a man and woman.

Pioneer spaceprobe

Gold-plated record with "Sounds of Earth" and cover for *Voyager 1*.

The record was mounted on a bracket on *Voyager 1*.

A record into space

The *Voyager 1* and *2*, both sent up in 1977, each carried a gold-plated LP record, a disc that has encoded sounds and photographs that will provide an alien intelligence with an idea of life on the Earth. There are greetings in 56 languages – and that includes a recording of whale song.

Turn and learn

Radio telescopes: **pp. 12-13**
Other Earths: **pp. 100-101**

93

Is there life on Mars?

Historically, many people have believed that a race of creatures live on Mars. Representations have appeared in books, artwork, comics, on the radio, on television and in films, in many different forms. Do any of these creatures actually exist? No!

A big prize!

In 1900, the French Guzman prize offered an award of 100,000 francs for the first person to make contact with extraterrestrials. Terms actually excluded contact with Martians as it was believed to be too easy!

Camille Flammarion's (founder of the Société Astronomique) "Flat Earth" woodcut influenced Clara Goguet Guzman to offer the prize.

Two hundred years ago

In the 1780s, William Herschel observed seasonal changes around the Martian poles and noted that its inhabitants "probably enjoy a situation in many respects similar to our own".

William Herschel

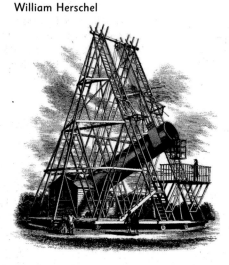

Herschel's 12-m (40-ft) telescope

In the papers

In the 1920s, a newspaper report on the Martians claimed they would have "very large noses and ears and immense lung development... Their legs are poorly developed, because matter on Mars weighs less than here".

94

One hundred years ago

The idea of intelligent Martian life reached a peak at the turn of the 20th century, when a wealthy businessman, Percival Lowell (1855–1916), set up his own observatory in Arizona, USA, and began to study Mars.

Lowell claimed he could see a network of lines criss-crossing the surface of Mars, which he believed were built to transport water from the poles around the planet.

Martians sell books

We now know the lines weren't there, but many people believed Lowell's theories, caught up by the excitement of the idea. The discussions inspired H. G. Wells' *The War of the Worlds* – a book published in 1898.

Illustration from H. G. Wells' book *The War of the Worlds*.

In 1938, a radio dramatization of H. G. Wells' book by Orson Welles frightened around one million Americans because it described the Martian invasion of the Earth in the form of a news report.

He claimed to have seen an incredible 585!

The Big Bang

A Universe is born

Georges Lemaitre

What was later termed the Big Bang was first proposed by Georges Lemaître in 1931. Scientists believe it was the beginning of everything, but don't know what caused it to happen.

Most scientists now believe that the Universe was born from a hot, dense spot more than 13 billion years ago. They call this event the Big Bang.

As the Universe expands and cools, at 300,000 years, matter as we know it starts to form. The Universe is a thousandth of its size today.

What happened?

Space and time were brought to life from a minute speck, which was unbelievably hot and heavy. The energy contained in this speck immediately began to spread out, in the form of an ever expanding fireball.

The Big Bang — "a day without yesterday".

What device did Arno Penzias and Robert Wilson use to detect Cosmic Background Radiation?

A long time coming

Matter only began to form hundreds of thousands of years after the Big Bang – long after the fireball had cooled. The resulting gases would form the stars, planets, and galaxies that exist today.

At 9 billion years, the Universe looks much as it does today, if a little bit smaller. Our Sun starts to form.

Stars and galaxies start to form after about 300 million years.

What's that?

Scientists have detected a faint radio signal, present in any direction they look for it in space. They believe it is a faint glow from the Big Bang's superhot fireball. It is called The Cosmic Background Radiation.

The Cosmic Background Radiation was discovered by American physicists Arno Penzias and Robert Wilson in the 1960s.

No beginning, no end

An alternative to the Big Bang, the Steady State Theory claimed there was no beginning or end for the Universe. It's just always been there. Few scientists now believe in the Steady State Theory.

weird or what?
The astronomer who gave the Big Bang theory its name didn't support it. He termed it Big Bang as a criticism and was surprised that the name stuck. He believed in the Steady State Theory.

Black holes

Black holes are a great mystery. Astronomers know they are there because of their effect on nearby stars (if a star is too close, it gets pulled towards the hole), but they are very difficult to study. Why? Because they are black, and that makes them invisible!

When Sun-like stars are dying, they push off their outer layers (right). More massive stars can explode and form a black hole.

Sometimes, some of the falling gas is squirted back out as hot jets.

This artist's idea of a black hole shows clouds of gas and dust swirling rapidly around it before being pulled in towards the hole at the centre.

Birth of a hole

Black holes are sometimes born when a star explodes and dies. When a star with great mass runs out of fuel, it can't stop gravity pulling its gas together, squeezing it tighter and tighter until it forms a tiny neutron star, or a black hole.

Into the hole

Black holes have such strong gravity that nothing in the surrounding space can escape, not even light. However, they do not act as enormous vacuum cleaners – something has to get close enough to be in danger of being pulled in. They are a bit like space whirlpools, affecting just their area of space.

98

How big can a black hole get?

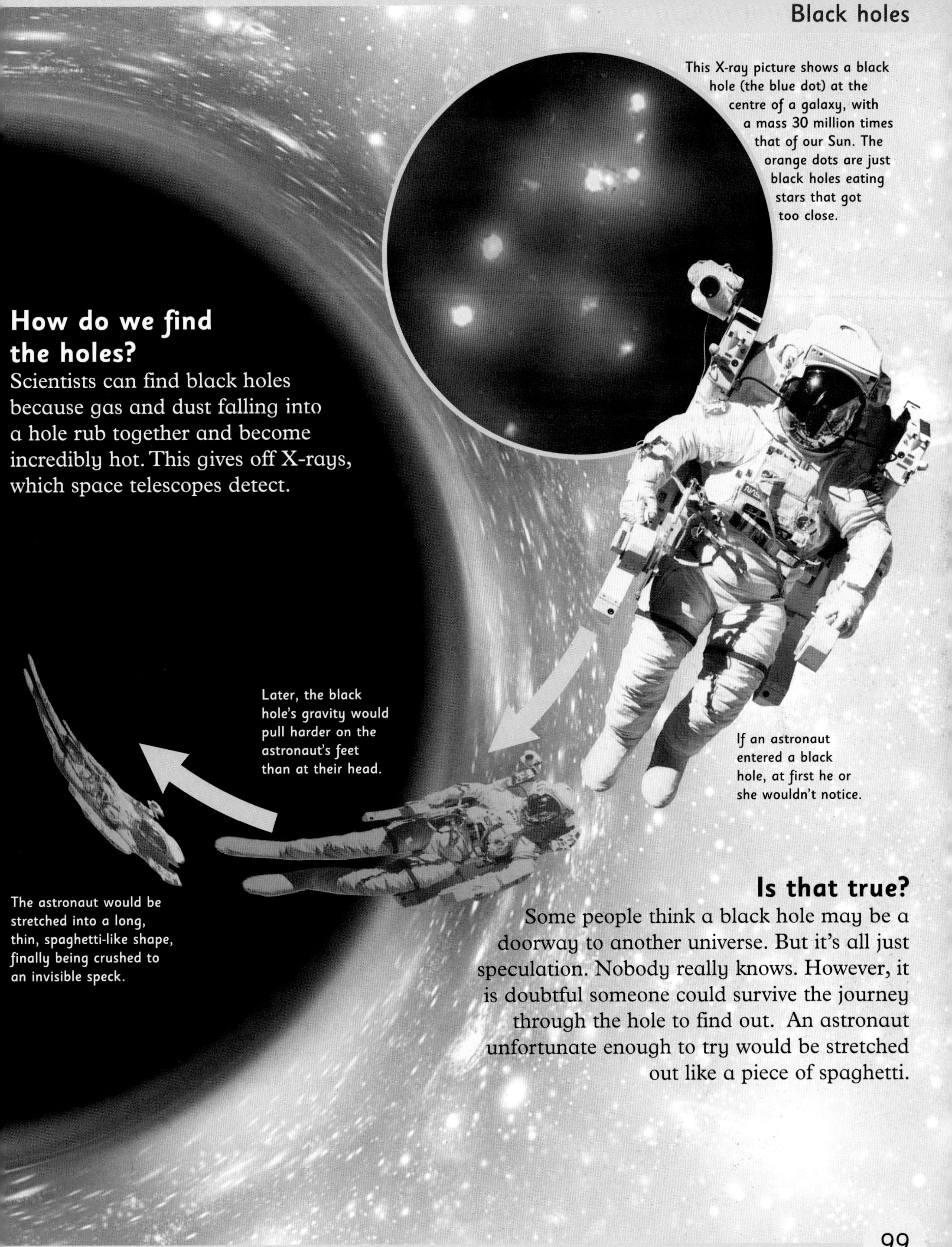

This X-ray picture shows a black hole (the blue dot) at the centre of a galaxy, with a mass 30 million times that of our Sun. The orange dots are just black holes eating stars that got too close.

How do we find the holes?

Scientists can find black holes because gas and dust falling into a hole rub together and become incredibly hot. This gives off X-rays, which space telescopes detect.

Later, the black hole's gravity would pull harder on the astronaut's feet than at their head.

If an astronaut entered a black hole, at first he or she wouldn't notice.

The astronaut would be stretched into a long, thin, spaghetti-like shape, finally being crushed to an invisible speck.

Is that true?

Some people think a black hole may be a doorway to another universe. But it's all just speculation. Nobody really knows. However, it is doubtful someone could survive the journey through the hole to find out. An astronaut unfortunate enough to try would be stretched out like a piece of spaghetti.

They grow as they "eat", so they are only limited in size by the matter they consume.

Are there other Earths?

Astronomers know that there are planets outside our solar system. One day they hope to discover a planet that is capable of supporting life. The search has begun.

An important discovery

About 20 light years away from us lies a star called Gliese 581. Astronomers have identified three planets orbiting Gliese. A planet too close to its star will be too hot for life, and the one too far away will be too cold. However, the one in the "Goldilocks", or habitable, zone could be just right.

Gliese 581 is a red dwarf.

Gliese 581e takes 3.15 days to orbit its sun and is likely to be too hot to support life.

Gliese 581b takes 5.4 days to orbit its sun, and may be the right distance from it to support life.

Gliese 581c may be rocky – or it may be composed of gas. Nobody is really sure.

How right?

At first, experts thought Gliese 581c was in the Goldilocks zone, where surface temperatures would allow liquid water. Now however, they believe there may be a fourth, more distant planet.

When was the first sun-like exoplanet discovered?

Compared to the Earth

The planets we find are so distant that it is difficult to be sure of their size or their composition.

12,742 km (7,918 miles)

20,000 km (12,428 miles)

Gliese 581c is thought to be about 20,000 km (12,428 miles) across, with a mass about five times that of the Earth.

The outline represents Gliese 581c.

Gliese 581c takes 15 days to orbit its sun and lies outside the habitable zone.

Exoplanet HD 189733b was discovered in 2005 as it dimmed the light of its parent star when passing in front of it.

Are there others?

Exoplanets are planets orbiting a star other than our Sun. About 2,000 have been identified since the first one was discovered in 1992. Astronomers believe there are many more. Exoplanets cannot be seen through a telescope. One way they are found is by looking for a star's "wobble", or shift in the colour of its light, as it is affected by an orbiting planet.

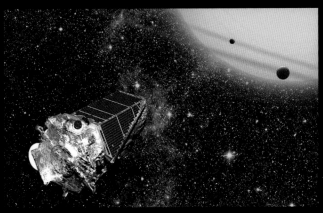

The quest for habitable planets

The *Kepler* spacecraft was launched by NASA in 2009 to discover Earth-like planets orbiting other stars. It has discovered more than 1,000 exoplanets, or extrasolar planets, in our region of the Milky Way.

Other space telescopes that are looking for planets include Europe's *CoRoT* satellite, seen here before launch. It worked from 2007 to 2013, and in that time discovered 32 exoplanets.

101

1995.

A star is born

Like many space pictures, this image of the Eagle Nebula has been artificially coloured so it can be seen clearly.

Clusters of stars are constantly being born from clouds of gas and dust thousands of times the size of our solar system, in a process that can take millions of years.

Born in a cloud

Between existing stars, there are patches of gas and dust. Gradually, these draw in more and more gas and dust to form huge clouds called nebulae.

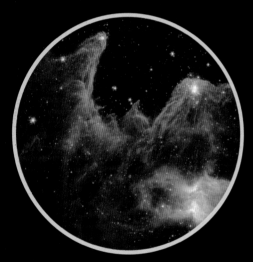

Nebula

Hot colours

As the matter within gets more and more dense, the clouds start to shrink under their own gravity, and eventually break into clumps. This collapse builds up heat, which forms a dense, hot core (protostar) that fills the surrounding nebulae with light and colour. This spectacular effect (right) was captured by the *Spitzer* space telescope.

The process of star formation captured by the *Hubble* telescope.

We have fusion!

With enough matter, the process of heating continues. The core gets denser and hotter. Eventually nuclear fusion begins, releasing huge amounts of heat and light – a star is born.

Which star cluster is also called the Seven Sisters?

What's in a name?

Horsehead, Lagoon, Eagle, and Crab... some of the best-known nebulae have popular names inspired by their shape.

Crab Nebula

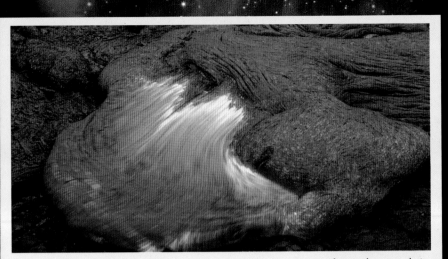

Is that one red?

Some stars shine red, others shine yellow or bluish white. A star's colour depends on its temperature. Red stars are the coolest, while blue stars are the hottest.

Lava also reveals its temperature through its colour. Here, the yellow lava is hotter than the red.

Our Sun is a yellow dwarf star. These stars are medium-sized, and live about 10 billion years.

What type of star?

Stars have different characteristics according to the amount of matter involved in their birth. They differ in colour, temperature, and brightness, and in the length of time they stay alive.

The life of a star

The Universe is home to lots of different types of star.

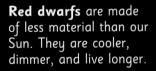

Red dwarfs are made of less material than our Sun. They are cooler, dimmer, and live longer.

Blue giants are among the hottest stars, and live for less than 100 million years.

Supergiants are the rarest stars. They have short lives – under 50 million years.

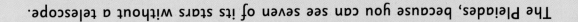

The Pleiades, because you can see seven of its stars without a telescope.

Death of a star

Stars are born, live out their lives, and, ultimately, die. In dying, all their elements are thrown back into the clouds of gas and dust from which they formed, and the process begins again.

Artist's impression of our Sun losing its outer layers at the end of its life

The Moon

Moon of planet below

Getting bigger...

When a star such as our Sun gets old, it begins to expand. It becomes a red giant or supergiant. This is because as it uses up its fuel – hydrogen – its centre or core becomes smaller and hotter. That leads to its expansion.

The surface of a planet whose sky is filled with a red giant star

did you know?
We are made from elements such as oxygen, hydrogen, carbon, and iron. While hydrogen has been around since time began, other elements form inside stars and spread when they die.

How much longer will our Sun continue to burn its hydrogen?

... and finally smaller

Once it's hot enough, a red giant starts to burn a new fuel called helium. That pushes the outer layers of the star further out. The star then begins to lose these layers as a nebula, and eventually emerges as a small, white dwarf star.

All living things are made from stardust.

The Earth

Going out with a bang

Some giant stars end their lives with a huge explosion, called a supernova. Sometimes the centre will survive as a black hole or neutron star.

A giant star pictured before it exploded and formed the supernova 1987a.

1987a was the brightest supernova in the Earth's skies for almost four centuries.

A lighthouse in space

Some neutron stars send out radio waves that sweep around as the star spins. Astronomers can pick up these signals. These neutron stars are called pulsars.

Images of dying stars

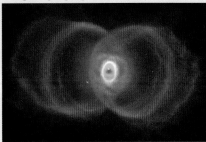

This is the young Hourglass Nebula (MyCn18) around a dying star.

Here's an example of a butterfly nebula showing its supersonic "exhaust".

A star's spectacular death in the constellation Taurus, which was observed as supernova 1054.

Its fuel will last another five billion years.

Space for everyone

The Sun has set. It's a clear night, and the stars are beginning to appear. Why not go outside and enjoy a bit of astronomy! It's fascinating. It's easy to do. And the more you look, the more you will see.

What do you need?

You don't need special equipment to study the stars – about 2,500 stars are visible to the naked eye in a clear sky, but you will find that binoculars help you to pick out more.

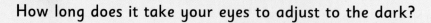
How long does it take your eyes to adjust to the dark?

Constellations

You will soon be spotting constellations. This is a part of the constellation of Sagittarius.

Orion's belt

There are lots of constellations. One of the easiest to pick out is Orion – by spotting the three bright stars that make up this hunter's belt.

Picture detective
Look through the Space for Everyone section and see if you can identify the pictures below.

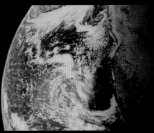

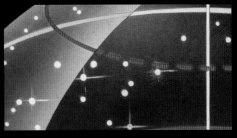

Light pollution

Streetlamps and the light from cars and houses all make the sky brighter, which makes it harder to see. But you can still see the Moon and main constellations. If you are lucky, you may see a comet or a meteor.

Turn and learn
Stargazing:
pp. 108-109
Constellations:
pp. 112-113

It takes about 30 minutes, especially if you have been in a lit room.

Become a stargazer

So you've decided to take a look at the night sky. What will you need to get you going? What should you look for? Here are a few tips to help get you started.

Basic equipment
Here is a selection of the basic equipment you might find helpful.

Torch

Torchlight tip
If you need to look at a star map while outside, cover the end of your torch in red cellophane. Red light doesn't interfere so much with night vision as white light.

Make notes
It's helpful to note what you have observed. Note the time, year, date, weather conditions, and location. Use a compass if you can, so you know the direction you are looking in.

Compass

Binoculars

It's an 8 x 30!
Binoculars are sold in different sizes and powers. The numbers tell you what they are. The first tells you by how many times the binoculars will magnify an object. The second is the measurement in millimetres across the front lenses.

Star maps
It may be worth buying a planisphere. This is a circular map of the stars, made from two plastic discs. Line up the date and time and the discs reveal the stars that can be seen.

An ancient skill
Astronomy is the study of the Universe. The word "astronomy" comes from two Greek words – *astron*, meaning "star", and *nemein*, meaning "to name".

Larger lenses gather more light, but the larger the lens, the heavier the binoculars.

Holding binoculars steady while looking at the night sky can make your arms ache. Try to find something on which you can rest your arms.

Can you name some of the well-known constellations?

What's the story?

Many constellations were named after characters in ancient Greek myth. Orion (seen here) was named because ancient astronomers imagined two lines of stars picked out this hunter's belt and sword.

The 12 constellations of the zodiac lie on an imaginary band in the sky.

The zodiac

This is an imaginary band within which the Sun, Moon, and planets appear to travel. The band has 12 divisions, and each part is a constellation. The name zodiac comes from the Greek word *zōidiakos* which means "circle of animals", although not all 12 are animals.

Close neighbours

A constellation's stars are not as close together as they appear. This diagram of the Cassiopeia constellation shows how the distances vary.

Are you north or south?

The sphere of the sky is divided into two halves – the northern and southern celestial hemispheres. Star maps show the location of constellations as they can be seen from each hemisphere. However, which stars you can see depends on where you live on the Earth.

The closest star in the Cassiopeia constellation is just over 50 light years away. The most distant is more than 600 light years away.

The northern sky

A star map of the northern sky is a flattened picture that shows some of the constellations seen from the northern hemisphere (that's anywhere north of the equator). Choose a clear night and look up. If you live near the equator, you won't be able to spot all these stars all year.

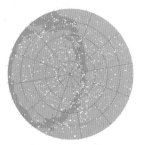

A star map of the northern sky

Imagine the Earth surrounded by a sphere of stars. The northern sky map is taken from the top half of that sphere.

Which way?

Travellers in the northern hemisphere can easily find their way by following Polaris, or the North Star, because it lies almost directly above the North Pole. If you spot Polaris, you will know which way is north and can work out which way you need to go.

As the Earth turns, Polaris stays put in the sky because it is above the North Pole. The other stars appear to travel round it.

Ursa Major

Polaris

Camelopardalis

Cassiopeia

Which distinctive constellation is used as a "signpost" in the northern sky?

Start spotting the constellations

You'll find it soon becomes easy to pick out more constellations than those shown. Some, such as the well-known hunter Orion, are visible in both northern and southern skies.

The Great Bear

In Roman mythology, Ursa Major (the Great Bear) represents Callisto, a beautiful girl who was turned into a bear by Juno, the wife of Jupiter – king of the gods in Roman mythology.

Ursa Major

Cameleopardalis

This constellation was named in 1613, which was only some 400 years ago – that's relatively recent for a constellation. It represents a giraffe.

Cameleopardalis

Draco

Ursa Minor

Cepheus

Cepheus

This constellation is said to show a mythical Greek king, who stands next to his wife, Cassiopeia.

Cepheus

115

The southern sky

This star map shows some of the constellations in the southern hemisphere (that's anywhere south of the equator). Look up at the sky on a clear night. You might not be able to see all these stars all year round if you live close to the equator.

A star map of the southern sky

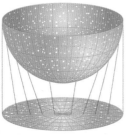

Imagine the Earth surrounded by a sphere of stars. The southern sky map is taken from the bottom half of that sphere.

They won't stay still!

As you begin star-spotting you will notice that the stars and constellations don't appear to be fixed in the same place. This is because the Earth's rotation makes the stars appear to move.

The stars' apparent movement shows clearly on a long exposure photograph of the night sky.

Centaurus

Crux

Pavo

Which distinctive constellation is used as a "signpost" in the southern sky?

Spotting the constellations

The more stargazing you do, the easier it becomes to pick out constellations. Here are a few that you can look for in southern skies.

Phoenix

Phoenix

This is a mythical bird that burns itself up when it reaches the end of its life, and is then reborn from its ashes. The constellation was named in the 1600s.

Pavo

This constellation is said to represent a peacock. Its brightest star, which represents the peacock's neck, is called Peacock.

Pavo

Centaurus

This constellation was named by the ancient Greek astronomer Ptolemy, and forms one of the largest of all constellations. It represents the centaur – a mythical creature that is half-man, half-horse.

Centaurus

Chamaeleon

Dorado

Phoenix

117

The Crux (otherwise known as the Southern Cross).

Space technology

Some of the inventions we use today are closely connected to the space program. Just take a look at the following.

A hand-held Dustbuster has super-suction power.

Cordless tools

Space scientists and power-tool designers together made cordless tools so astronauts could drill rocks on the Moon. This work led to the invention of cordless medical instruments and a cordless vacuum cleaner.

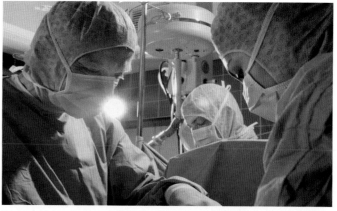

Surgeons use lightweight, battery-powered instruments.

Medical scans

Computer software, originally designed to enhance pictures of the Moon, is now used by medical staff. It makes scans of the human body easy to read so doctors can diagnose diseases.

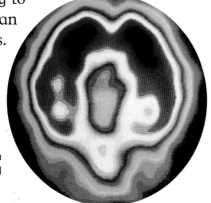

Scan of a human head

Memory foam

This was developed to improve seating and crash protection for pilots. The foam moulds to the shape of the body, then returns to its original shape.

Memory foam is used here in a neck cushion.

118

What is "memory foam" also known as?

Aerodynamic bicycle wheel

Following research, three-spoked bicycle wheels were developed into shapes that move quickly and easily.

These wheels maximize the bikes' efficiency for racing.

Material facts

Some people believe these materials were invented for the space program, when in fact they were just used by it. The heat-resistant plastic, Teflon, for example, was invented in 1938 and later used on space suits and heat shields.

Teflon is commonly used as a non-stick covering for cooking pans. It is also a stain-resistant fabric protector.

Velcro was invented in the 1940s and later used during the Apollo missions to hold tools and equipment in place at zero gravity, when they would otherwise have floated off. It is now used on the International Space Station. Velcro is also used to secure clothing.

Things like these

During the 1960s onwards, US space agency NASA adapted everyday objects for use in its space program.

NASA made its own smoke detector with adjustable sensitivity. It also used smoke detectors on Skylab, the space station launched in 1973, to detect toxic vapours.

ISBN 1-4053-1037-5

9 781405 310376

A type of bar coding was used by NASA to keep track of spacecraft components.

Quartz clocks were first used in the 1920s. In the 1960s, NASA worked to produce a highly accurate quartz clock.

Temper foam.

Space timeline

Since humankind began exploring space in the 1950s, there have been a number of key moments. From the first satellite to the launch of the International Space Station, take a look at some of these amazing events.

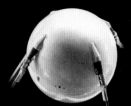
Sputnik 1

1957
The first man-made satellite, *Sputnik 1*, took approximately 98 minutes to orbit the Earth.

1957
The first living creature was sent into orbit – Laika the dog was strapped into *Sputnik 2*.

Luna 3 was a Soviet spacecraft.

1959
We had our first glimpse of the far side of the Moon from the *Luna 3* spacecraft.

1961
The first human in space was Yuri Gagarin, whose orbit of the Earth lasted 108 minutes.

1963
The first woman in space was Valentina Tereshkova on *Vostok 6*. The flight lasted 70 hours, 50 minutes and orbited the Earth 48 times.

1965
The first spacewalk, lasting about 10 minutes, was achieved by Alexei Arkhipovich Leonov.

1969
The first human to step on the Moon was Neil Armstrong from *Apollo 11*. The other crew member who walked on the Moon was Edward "Buzz" Aldrin.

Astronaut Buzz Aldrin walks on the Moon.

What was the name of the third astronaut on the Apollo 11 mission?

The International Space Station

1973

The first US space station, Skylab, went into orbit. It was to be manned by three successive crews who would perform nearly 300 experiments while on board. Skylab fell back to the Earth in 1979.

1977

Voyager 2 is launched, closely followed by *Voyager 1*. The spacecraft have studied the solar system's outer planetary systems, and are still operating.

1986

The first section of Mir, the Russian space station, was launched. Mir was the first permanent residence in space and was almost continuously occupied until 2000. Mir burnt up in the Earth's atmosphere, after 15 years in orbit, in 2001.

Lift-off of
Titan III-Centaur
vehicle carrying
Voyager 2

1998

The first part of the International Space Station (ISS) was launched. Still in operation today, it is powered by large solar panels and orbits the Earth at an altitude of 360 km (225 miles).

2004

Cassini, the first craft to orbit Saturn, sends back the clearest photographs ever of Saturn's ring system. It continues to orbit the planet and its moons today.

2010

Developed by the Japan Aerospace Exploration Agency (JAXA), the spacecraft *Hayabusa* became the first to return asteroid samples to Earth. It had collected them from the asteroid Itokawa.

2015

NASA's *Dawn* spacecraft became the first to orbit a dwarf planet. It had completed a journey of 4.9 billion km (3.1 billion miles) and seven and a half years, before going into orbit around Ceres.

Mir space station

***Dawn* spacecraft**

Michael Collins.

True or false?

Can you work out which of these facts are real, and which ones are completely made up?

4 Halley's comet travels past the Earth every 50 years.

1 There are 100 internationally recognised constellations.

5 NASA astronauts spend two years in basic training.

2 Meteorites have a high iron content that attracts magnets.

3 The Apollo missions were the first to use Velcro in space.

6: False – it is named after the god of war 7: True 8: False – they detect radio waves 9: True

6 The planet Mars is named after the Roman goddess of love.

7 The Hubble Space Telescope is controlled from the Earth.

8 Radio telescopes are used to detect ultraviolet rays coming from space.

9 The Saturn V is the largest, most powerful rocket ever built.

123

Answers. 1: False – there are 88 2: True 3: True 4: False – every 75 or 76 years 5: True

Quiz

Test your knowledge
with these quiz questions.

1 To which planet was the *Opportunity* rover sent
to collect data?

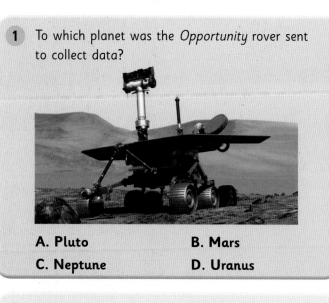

A. Pluto   **B. Mars**
C. Neptune   **D. Uranus**

2 "Morning star" is another name for which planet?

A: Saturn   **B: Mercury**
C: Earth   **D: Venus**

3 How long does it take the Earth to orbit the Sun?

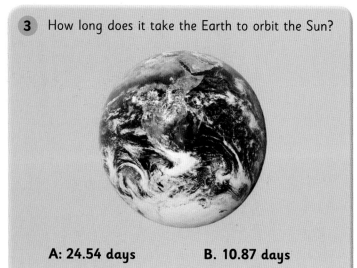

A: 24.54 days   **B. 10.87 days**
C. 365.25 days   **D. 243.47 days**

4 After the Sun, which star is closest to the Earth?

A. Barnard's Star   **B. Polaris**
C. Proxima Centauri   **D. Gliese 581**

5 A supernova occurs when a star...

A. Is dying   **B. Is born**
C. Burns hydrogen   **D. Burns helium**

6 How many planets in our solar system have
rings around them?

A. 5   **B. 1**
C. 4   **D. 3**

7 What are the twin Keck telescopes designed
to detect?

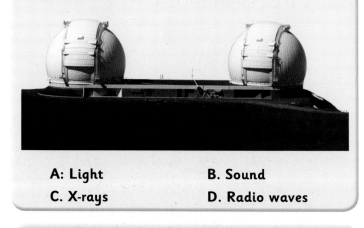

A: Light   **B. Sound**
C. X-rays   **D. Radio waves**

8 The first liquid-filled rocket was created by...

A. Buzz Aldrin   **B. Robert Goddard**
C. Alexei Leonov   **D. Galileo Galilei**

9 It is not possible to land a spacecraft on Saturn because it has...

A: Large craters B: Active volcanoes
C: No solid surface D: Ice

10 Binoculars with larger lenses are recommended for a stargazer because they...

A: Gather more light B: Are inexpensive
C: Are easy to carry D: Have better focus

11 What kind of satellite is Ganymede?

A: Resource satellite B: Weather satellite
C: Natural satellite D: Military satellite

12 In which part of the Earth's atmosphere do the polar lights occur?

A: Mesosphere B: Troposphere
C: Exosphere D: Thermosphere

13 Which part of the *Apollo 11* actually landed on the Moon?

A: Lunar module B: Rocket engine
C: Command module D: Service module

14 A nebula is a cloud in space made up of...

A: Gas and vapour B: Ice and vapour
C: Dust and ice D: Gas and dust

15 When did the first spacewalk take place?

A. July 1950 B. August 1960
C. June 1965 D. March 1965

16 The Galileo spacecraft's mission was to orbit and study...

A. Itokawa B. Phobos
C. Helix Nebula D. Jupiter

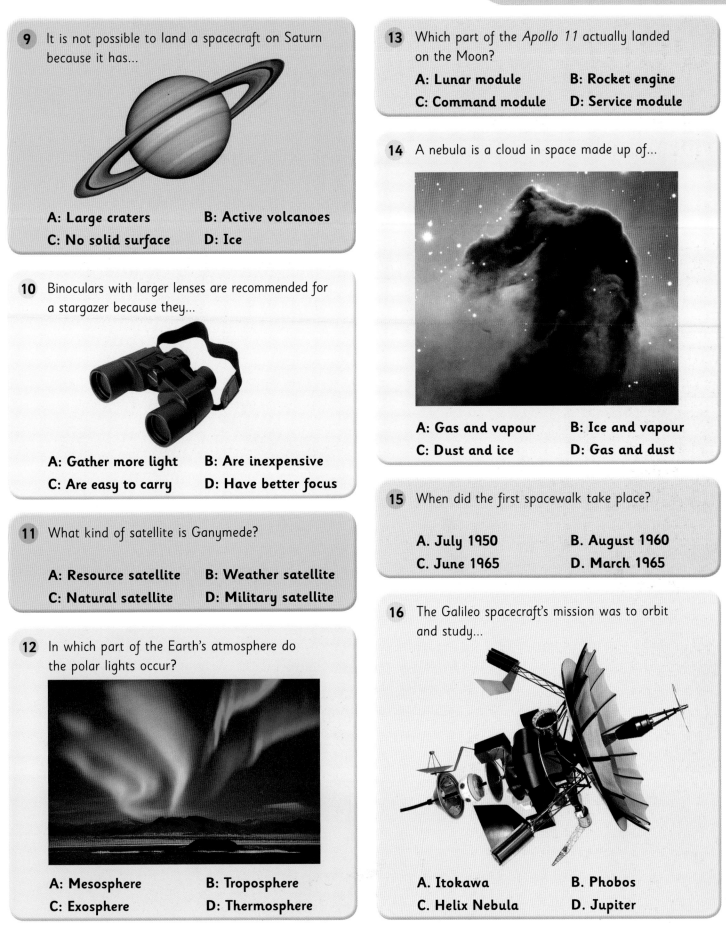

Answers: 1:B 2:D 3:C 4:C 5:A 6:C 7:A 8:B 9:C 10:A 11:C 12:D 13:A 14:D 15:D 16:D

What am I?

Can you work out what is being talked about from the clue?

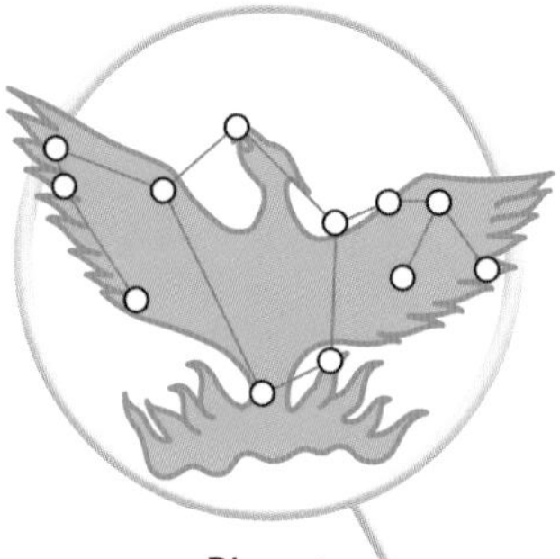

Phoenix

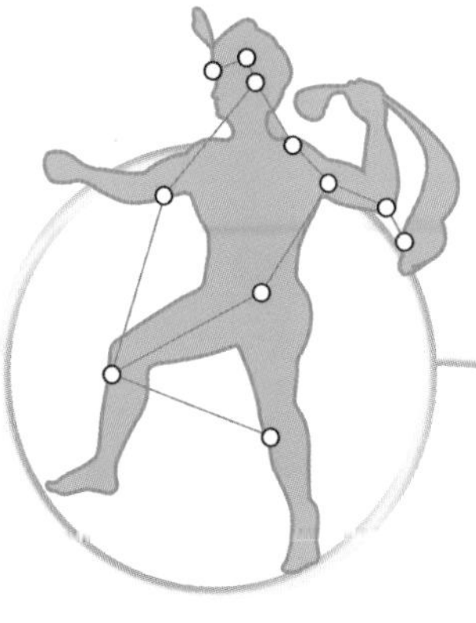

Cepheus

2: I am a constellation that was named in 1613.

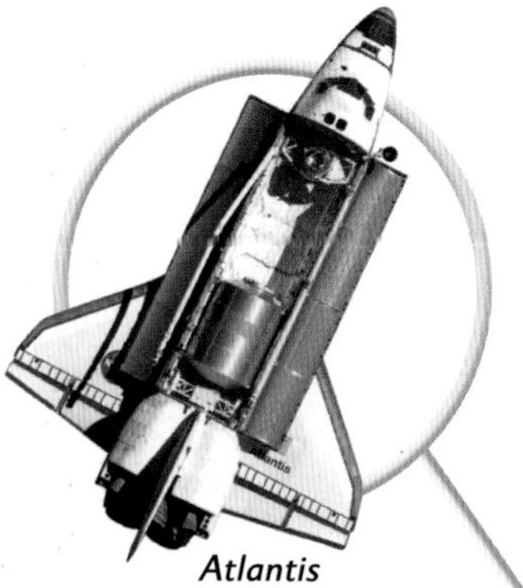

Atlantis

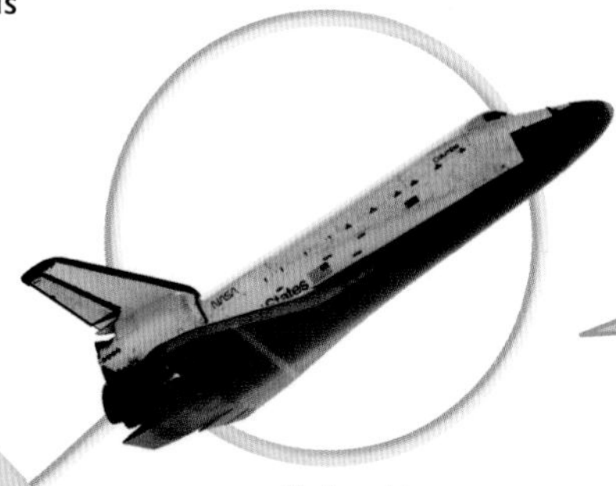

Columbia

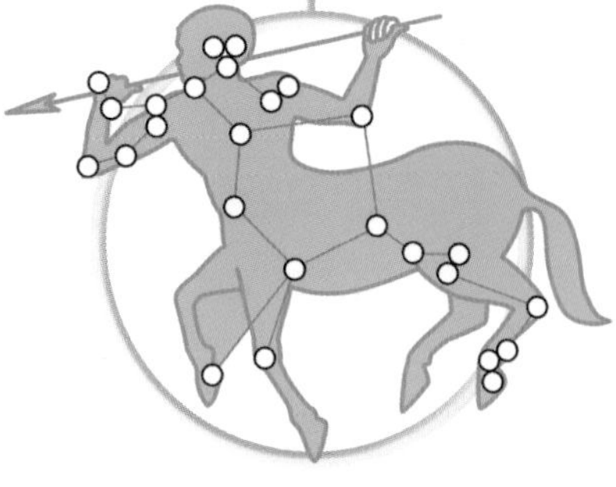

Centaurus

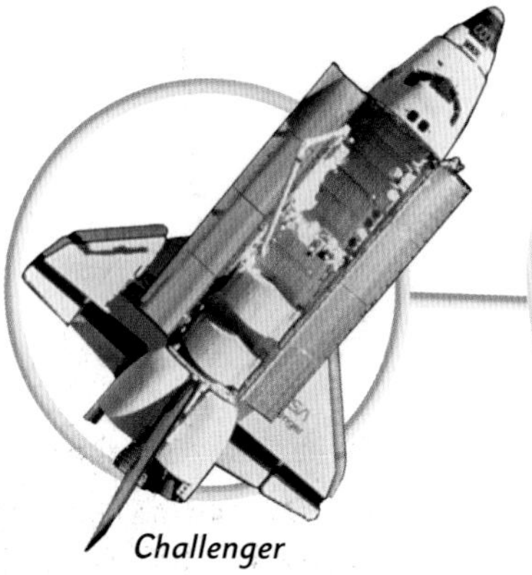

1: I am a space shuttle that disintegrated during re-entry in 2003.

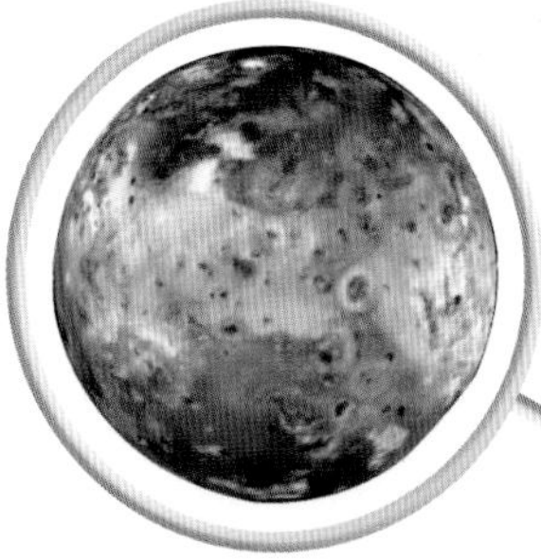

Challenger

Io

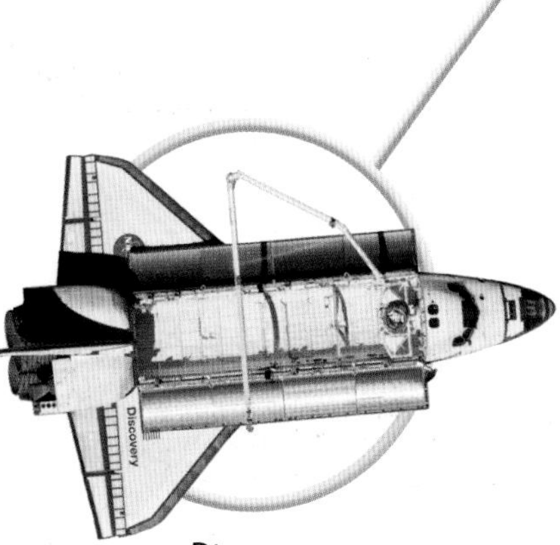

Discovery

Endeavour

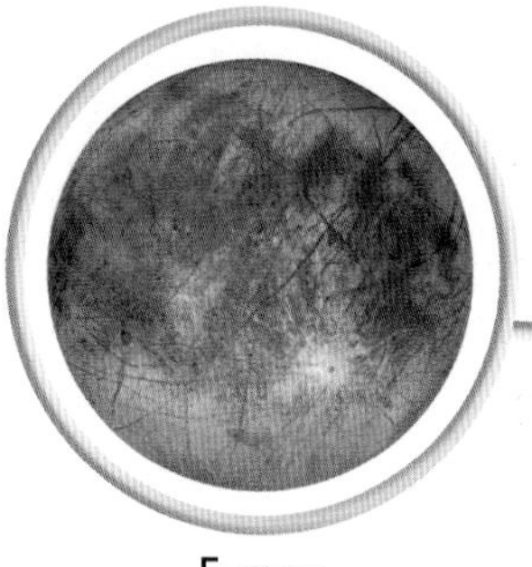

Europa

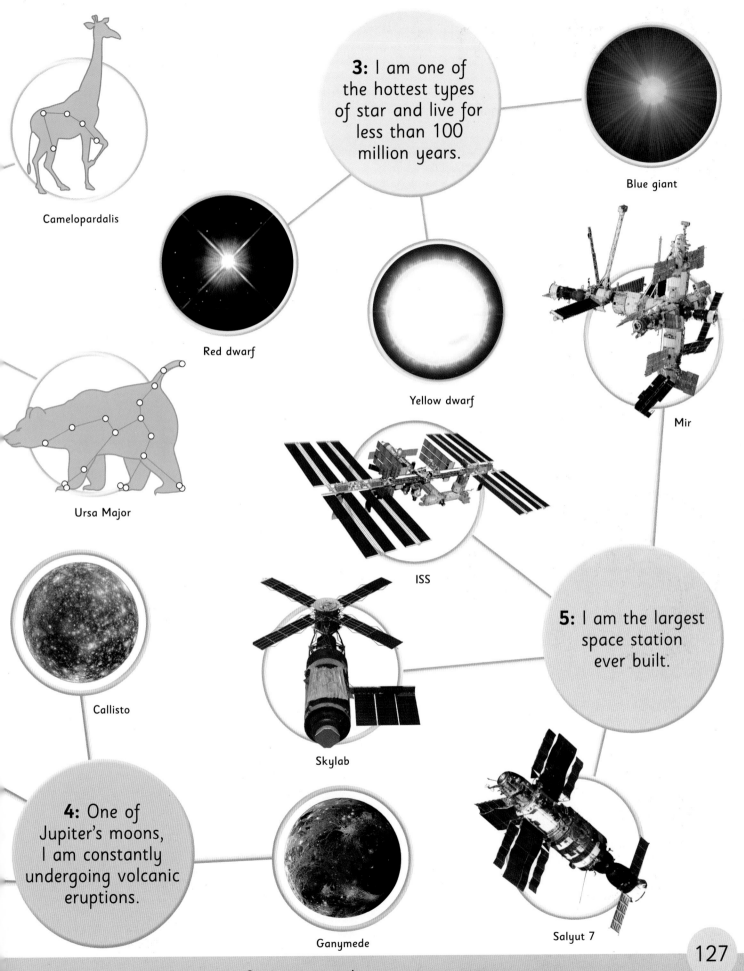

Camelopardalis

3: I am one of the hottest types of star and live for less than 100 million years.

Blue giant

Red dwarf

Yellow dwarf

Mir

Ursa Major

ISS

Callisto

Skylab

5: I am the largest space station ever built.

4: One of Jupiter's moons, I am constantly undergoing volcanic eruptions.

Ganymede

Salyut 7

127

3: This planet was originally named George's Star, after the British King George III.

2: This US astronaut was the first person to set foot on the Moon.

4: This radio telescope was used to send a message towards a cluster of stars called M13.

1: Fragments of the Canon Diablo meteorite were found in this crater in Arizona, USA.

5: This planet was named after the Roman god of the sea.

Where in the world?

Test your knowledge about where each of these come from or are found by matching the clues to the pictures.

Barringer Crater

Neptune

Neil Armstrong

Parkes telescope

Luna 3

Nicolaus Copernicus

7: Galileo Galilei 8: Yuri Gagarin 9: Luna 3 10: Hayabusa 11: Parkes telescope 12: Wolf Creek Crater

6: This Polish astronomer was the first to suggest that the Earth orbits around the Sun.

9: This spacecraft was made in the Soviet Union and took the first pictures of the far side of the Moon.

8: This Russian became the first man to go into space in 1961.

10: This Japanese spacecraft was sent to collect samples from the asteroid Itokawa.

7: This Italian scientist built a simple telescope in 1609.

12: This meteor crater in Western Australia was formed between one and two million years ago.

11: This radio telescope was used by SETI to search for alien life.

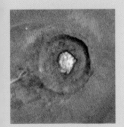

Wolf Creek Crater

Galileo Galilei

Hayabusa

Arecibo telescope

Yuri Gagarin

Uranus

129

Answers: 1: Barringer Crater 2: Neil Armstrong 3: Neptune 4: Uranus 5: Arecibo telescope 6: Nicolaus Copernicus

Glossary

asteroid Giant rock, also called a minor planet or planetoid, that circles the Sun. There are hundreds of thousands in our solar system and more are being discovered all the time

astronaut Person who has been trained to travel inside a spacecraft

astronomy Branch of science that studies the places beyond the Earth such as stars, planets, comets, and galaxies

atmosphere Thin layer of gas surrounding the Earth for about 100 km (63 miles), which fades gradually into space beyond

comet Space snowball made of dust, rock, and ice that orbits the Sun. Comets develop a bright head and tail when near the Sun

dwarf planet Celestial body too small to be considered a planet, and orbits the Sun amongst other objects

galaxy Large system of stars, gas, dust, and empty space that rotates but is held together by gravity. The Earth and its solar system are part of a galaxy called the Milky Way

gas Freely moving atoms or particles without a definite shape

black hole Area with a gravitational pull so strong that it sucks in anything that comes too close. Scientists know black holes exist because of their effect on nearby stars

gravity Attraction between everything in the Universe. Gravity makes the Earth and the other planets in the solar system orbit the Sun, and the Moon rotate around the Earth

light year Distance light travels in one year

meteor Short-lived streak of light produced by a small piece of space rock burning up in the Earth's atmosphere

meteorite Piece of space rock that survives the journey through the Earth's atmosphere and lands on its surface

moon Natural satellite, or an object orbiting a planet. The Earth has one moon, though more than 170 orbit other solar system planets

nebula Cloud of dust and gas in space that may eventually give birth to stars

observatory Any building or structure used to look into space. Optical observatories have a dome, often in a high-up location, housing a telescope. The roof can be opened to look at the sky. There are also radio observatories with big dishes, and space-based observatories (telescopes that orbit the Earth)

orbit Path an object makes around another object while under the influence of gravity

planet Large, round object orbiting a star

rocket Spacecrafts which carry satellites and people into space

satellite Object that orbits something larger than itself. The Moon is a natural satellite. Artificial satellites are objects put in orbit by humans

solar system Planets, moons, dwarf planets, comets, asteroids, and dust that orbit the Sun, held by its gravity

space Huge, largely empty areas in between the atmospheres of stars and planets. Space contains some dust and gas

spacecraft Vehicle or device designed to travel in space

space shuttle System used by the US government for 135 human space-flight missions from 1981 to 2011

space station Space laboratory orbiting the Earth, operated by crews of astronauts who live there for weeks or months

star Self-heating ball of glowing gas

Sun Star nearest to the Earth. It powers life on the Earth

telescope Instrument used to look at very distant things

UFO Unidentified flying objects are objects in the sky that people claim to have seen but cannot be identified. Some people cite them as evidence of life beyond the Earth

Universe Everything that exists – the Earth, Moon, Sun, all planets and all galaxies, and even those we haven't discovered yet

Index

cordless tools 118
CoRoT satellite 101
cosmonaut 24, 30
crop circles 90
Curiosity rover 46

D Daedalus 48
dark matter 23
Darwin telescope 101
Dawn spacecraft 121
Deimos (Mars's moon) 64
Delta 2 spacecraft 87
Discovery orbiter 37
dust 4, 14, 50, 64, 102
dwarf planet 14, 74-75, 83
dwarf star 21, 103

EF Earth 5, 6, 8, 14-15, 22, 34, 35, 50, 51, 53, 60-61, 62-63, 64, 66, 74, 87, 110
escape velocity 31
Extravehicular Mobility Unit (EMU) 28, 29
Endeavour orbiter 37
Enterprise spacecraft 49
Eros asteroid 84-85
Europa (Jupiter's moon) 50, 68-69
exoplanets 101
exosphere 6
fairing 7, 30
fuel tank 7, 31, 36

G Gagarin, Yuri 30, 120
Gaia satellite 7
galaxy 15, 16-17, 22, 97
Galilei, Galileo 8, 67, 68
Galileo telescope 67, 82, 83
Ganymede (Jupiter's moon) 50, 68-69
gas 4, 6, 14, 30, 60, 66, 72, 102
Gliese 581 star 100

B bar codes 119
Barnard's Star 48
bicycle wheels 119
Big Bang 88, 96-97
black hole 11, 98-99

C Callisto (Jupiter's moon) 50, 68-69
Camelopardalis 115
Cassini orbiter 121
Cassini-Huygens orbiter-probe 25, 71
Celestial sphere 112
Centaurus 117
Cepheus 115
Ceres 74-75, 83
Challenger orbiter 37, 87
Chandra telescope 11
Charon (Pluto's moon) 75
clothes 28, 29
Collins, Mike 34
Columbia orbiter 37
comet 14, 50, 56, 76-87
command module 32, 33, 34
constellations 106, 112-117
Copernicus 8

A air 7, 35
Aldrin, Buzz 34, 120
aliens 89, 92
Alpha Centauri 21
Apollo 11 spacecraft 32-33, 34, 35, 120
Ariane 5 rocket 30-31
Armstrong, Neil 33, 34, 35, 120
asteroid 14, 50, 75, 77, 82-83, 84-85
    Eros 84-85
    Itokawa 84
asteroid belt 50, 82-83
astronaut 4, 5, 24, 26-27, 28-29, 32, 33, 39, 40-41, 42-43, 99
astronomy 8, 106-118
Atlantis shuttle and orbiter 6, 37
atmosphere 6, 21, 35, 60, 64, 66, 72

gravity 4, 31, 40, 63, 82, 98, 99, 110
gravity assists 25
Great Dark Spot 73
Great Red Spot 66

H Halley's comet 78
Hayabusa 84
Helios 2 49
Hubble telescope 9
Hydra (Pluto's moon) 75

I International Space Station 29, 38, 42, 121
interstellar travel 48-49
Io (Jupiter's moon) 50, 67, 68-69
Itokawa asteroid 84

JK James Webb telescope 9
Jupiter 14, 50, 66-67, 68-69, 76
JAXA 121
Keck telescope 10
Kepler spacecraft 101

L Laika the dog 120
Leo 112
Leonids 81
Leonov, Alexei 43, 120
light year 4, 19, 20

Local Group 15, 16
Long March 2C rocket 30
Luna 3 probe 63, 120
Luna 9 probe 63
lunar module 32, 33
Lunar Prospector 63
Lunar Reconnaissance Orbiter 63
lunar rover 34

M *Magellan* probe 59
Mariner 10 probe 56
Marius, Simon 68, 69
Mars 14, 46-47, 50, 64-65, 94-95
Mars Express 46
Mars Reconnaissance Orbiter 46
Mars rovers 46, 47
medical instruments 118

Mercury 14, 50, 56-57, 61
mesosphere 6
MESSENGER probe 57
meteor 14, 56, 63, 76-87, 109
meteorite 77, 80
Milky Way 15, 16, 18-19, 22, 109
Mir space station 6, 38, 121
Miranda (Uranus's moon) 73
moons
    The Earth's moon 8, 14, 32-33, 34-35, 44, 49, 54, 55, 62-63, 74, 107, 110-111, 120
    Jupiter's moons 50, 67, 68-69
    Mars's moons 64
    Neptune's moons 73
    Pluto's moons 75
    Saturn's moons 71
    Uranus's moons 73
multiverse 23

N NASA 7, 26, 27, 37
NEAR-Shoemaker probe 84-85
nebula 4, 88, 102
Neptune 14, 50-51, 72, 73
Nix (Pluto's moon) 75
northern hemisphere 113,
   114-115
nose cone 7, 30

O observatories 10-11, 95
Opportunity rover 47
orbiter 7, 36
   Atlantis 6, 37
   Challenger 37, 87
   Columbia 37
   Discovery 37
   Endeavour 37
Orion 112, 113, 115
Orion Crew Vehicle 37
Orion's belt 106

P *Pathfinder* spacecraft 46
Pavo 117
payload 31
payload bay 26, 37
Perseids 109
Phobos (Mars's moon) 64
Phoenix 117
Pioneer probe 93
Pluto 14, 50, 51, 57, 74-75
probes
   Daedelus 48
   Huygens 25, 71
   Luna 3 63, 120
   Luna 9 63
   Lunar Prospector 63
   Lunar Reconnaissance Orbiter 63
   Magellan 59
   Mariner 10 56
   MESSENGER 57
   NEAR-Shoemaker 84-85
   Pioneer 93
   SOHO 52

TRACE 52
Ulysses 52
Promixa Centauri 20, 21, 49
pumpkin suit 28

R radio telescope 12-13,
   92-93
radio waves 12, 13
rocket 4, 30-31
   Ariane 5 30-31
   Delta 2 87
   Long March 2C 30
   Saturn V 31, 32
   Vostok 1 30
rocket booster 7, 36
rocket launcher 37
Roswell 91
rovers
   Curiosity 46
   Opportunity 47
   Sojourner 46
   Spirit 46-47

S Sagittarius 106
Salyut space station 38
satellite 4, 7, 14, 29, 30, 31, 44-45, 51,
   62, 120, 121
   CoRoT 101
   Gaia 7
   Sputnik 45, 120
   Telstar 44
Saturn 14, 25, 50-51, 70-71
Saturn V rocket 31, 32
service module 32, 33, 34
shooting stars 80-81
shuttle 6, 7, 29, 31, 36-37
Skylab space station 38, 121
SOHO probe 52
Sojourner rover 46
solar eclipse 54-55
solar system 14, 22, 50-75, 82-83
solar wind 52
Sojourner probe 46

southern hemisphere 113, 116-117
Soyuz spacecraft 31, 39
space probe 52, 56, 57, 63, 71, 84, 85, 93
space station 6, 29, 38-39, 120, 121
  Mir 6, 38, 121
  Salyut 38
  Skylab 38, 121
spacecraft 7, 24-25, 48, 71
  Apollo 11 32-33, 34, 35, 120
  Dawn 121
  Enterprise 49
  Galileo 67, 82, 83
  Hayabusa 84
  Helios 2 49
  Kepler 101
  Pathfinder 46
  Voyager 1 22, 24, 68, 93
  Voyager 2 73, 93, 121
spacewalk 42, 43
Spirit rover 46-47
Spitzer telescope 4, 102
Sputnik satellite 45, 120
stars 4, 11, 18, 20-21, 22, 52, 88, 97, 98, 100, 102-103, 104-105
stratosphere 6
Sun 4, 8, 14, 20, 22, 45, 50, 52-53, 54-55, 56, 58, 60, 66, 67, 72, 82, 97, 103
sunspot 52
supernova 88, 105

T Teflon 119
  telescope 8-9, 10-11, 12-13, 18, 88, 92-93, 99, 101
  Chandra 11
  Darwin 101
  Galileo 67, 82, 83
  Hubble 9
  James Webb 9
  Keck 10
  radio 12-13, 92-93
  Spitzer 4
Telstar satellite 44
Tereshkova, Valentina 120

thermosphere 6
Titan (Saturn's moon) 71
Titania (Uranus's moon) 73
TRACE probe 52
Triton (Neptune's moon) 73
troposphere 6

U UFOs 89, 90-91
  Ulysses probe 52
Universe 4, 8, 14, 22-23, 96-97
Uranus 14, 50-51, 72, 73
Ursa Major (Great Bear) 115

V velcro 119
  Venus 14, 50, 58-59, 61, 109
Vesta asteroid 83
Viking landers 46
Viking 1 Orbiter 65
volcano 10, 46, 59, 65
Vostok 1 rocket 30
Voyager 1 spacecraft 22, 24, 68, 93, 121
Voyager 2 spacecraft 73, 93, 121

WZ weightlessness 4, 27
  White, Edward 43
zodiac 113

Picture credits

The publisher would like to thank the following for their kind permission to reproduce their photographs:

(Key: a-above; b-below/bottom; c-centre; l-left; r-right; t-top)

Alamy Images: eStock Photo 56cla, 58tl, 64tl, 66tr, 70tr, 72tr, 75ca; Rab Harling 91bl; TNT Magazine 89cr; Richard Wainscoat 10-11b. **Bridgeman Art Library**: Victoria Art Gallery, Bath and North East Somerset Council 94cl. **Corbis**: 6bl, 19br, 35br, 35tc, 125b; Neil Armstrong 34 (Buzz Aldrin); Hinrich Baesemann/epa 52cl; Heide Benser 118cr; Bettmann 8cla, 25fcr, 28br, 33cb, 35clb, 35tr, 91br, 91cr; Bettmann/Neil Armstrong 34c; Bettmann/Paul Trent 90-91cb; Paul Chinn/San Francisco Chronicle 90cl; Richard Cummins 49t; Tim De Waele 119t; ESA/NASA 38-39c; Firefly Productions 11tl; Tim Kiusalaas 60cla; NASA 18tr, 60bl, 67tc, 110bl, 123br; NASA TV/ epa 29b; NASA TV/Handout/epa 39cr; NASA/ epa 37cra; NASA/JPL-Caltech 52br; NASA/ Roger Ressmeyer 18bl, 29tc; Roger Ressmeyer 77br (mission control), 87b, 107fcrb, 113tr, 118crb; Reuters 11tr, 38bl, 67cr; John Sevigny/ epa 70b; Jim Sugar 61cr; 127fbr Roger Ressmeyer. **DK Images**: Science Museum, London 8bl, 86tr, 118ftl; NASA 7bl, 44, 53tc, 69cb, 77clb (comet), 99cb, 99clb, 99cr, 101tl; 121ftl; NASA/Finley Holiday Films 68 (jupiter); NASA/JPL 51br, 66cl; Natural History Museum, London 80tl. **European Space Agency**: 7br, 9br, 31cr, 51cla, 101bl, 101tr; Studio - Bazile 101br. **Getty Images**: LWA 5tr, 19l; Riser/ Sightseeing Archive 34br; Antonio M Rosario 18cr; Space Frontiers/Dera 60-61c; Time & Life Pictures 121b. **JAXA**: ISAS 77crb (Itokawa), 84b, 84clb. **David Malin Images**: UK Schmidt Telescope/DSS/AAO 21r. **Mary Evans Picture Library**: 8l, 95tr. **NASA**: 1r, 4b, 4cl, 4cla, 4clb, 5bl, 5b, 6-7, 24br, 24fbr, 25br, 25fcra, 25fcrb, 25ftr, 26bl, 27b, 27r, 27tr, 28cb, 28clb, 28crb, 29tl (liferaft), 30ca, 31l, 31tr, 32tl, 36bl, 36r, 37b, 37cl, 37tl, 38cl, 39tl, 40cl, 40-41 (running machine), 41br, 41cla, 41clb, 41tr, 42tr, 42-43,

43b, 43cr, 43tr, 45bc, 45bl, 45c, 45ca, 45clb, 45crb, 45fclb, 45tr, 46br (polar lander), 46cr, 46cra (viking lander), 46crb, 46tl, 46-47 (b/g), 46-47b, 47br, 47cla, 47ftr, 47tr, 51fbr, 51tc, 51tl, 52bl, 52clb, 52fclb, 55br, 59tr, 64-65c, 68cr, 68ftr, 68tr, 69bc, 69ca, 69crb, 69l, 69tc, 69tc (false colour), 71tr, 72br, 72r, 73bc, 73bl, 73br, 73c, 73cla, 73clb, 73tr, 75br, 75cb, 77clb (asteroid), 77clb (meteorite), 79b, 83bc, 83cb, 88bc, 89cla, 89tr, 90cr, 93c, 93cr, 93cra, 102cl, 103cra, 103crb (yellow dwarf), 105cl, 105cr, 120tr, 124tl, 127, 128; ESA, H. Weaver-JHU/ APL, A. Stern-SwRI/HST Pluto Companion Search Team 75tr; ESA, K. Noll-STScI/ Hubble Heritage Team (STScI/AURA) 8-9t; GSFC 98c, 105fcr, 105fcra; H. Hammel, MIT 76bl; HQ-GRIN 89cr, 89fbr, 102br; JHUAPL/ Carnegie Institution of Washington 57bl; JPL 85ftr, 85tc, 85tr, 105fcrb; JSC 121tl; MSFC 84tl, 99tl, 105br (supergiant), 121ca, 121tr; D. Roddy (U.S. Geological Survey), Lunar and Planetary Institute 81cla (meteor crater). **National Radio Astronomy Observatory**: AUI/Dave Finley 13tl. **PunchStock**: Digital Archive Japan 52tl. **Science Photo Library**: 68bl, 71clb, 96tl; Mike Agliolo 78tl; David P. Anderson/SMU/NASA 58-59b; Julian Baum 42cra, 67bc, 76-77; Julian Baum/New Scientist 88-89; Sally Bensusen 54br; BMDO/NRL/ LLNL 51fcra, 63bl; Peter Bowater 45tl; Chris Butler 56-57b, 70cl, 74cl, 89cra, 104-105c; Celestial Image Co. 14br, 112l, 113r; China Great Wall Industry Corporation 30b; John Chumack 77tr, 79cr; Lynette Cook 82bl, 126bl; David Ducros 24-25; Bernhard Edmaier 77cra, 80bc; Hermann Eisenbeiss 62tr; Dr. Fred Espenak 12b, 54c, 109br; European Southern Observatory 100; European Space Agency 64cla, 71cb, 89br, 98bl; European Space Agency/DLR/FU Berlin/G. Neukum 65tr; John Foster 80-81; Mark Garlick 14tl, 19tr, 21b, 48-49b, 49cl, 74br, 74-75, 82-83c, 83tl, 96-97; Robert Gendler 14clb; David A. Hardy 25bl, 48clb; David A. Hardy, Futures: 50 Years In Space 16-17t, 104-105 (b/g); Adam Hart-Davis 47cr; Johns Hopkins University Applied Physics Laboratory 84-85cb; JPL-Caltech/STScI/

Vassar/NASA 5br, 14-15t; Manfred Kage 81clb (meteorite fragment); Mehau Kulyk 23br, 86bl, 98-99c; Larry Landolfi 4c, 51ca, 62-63; Dr. Michael J. Ledlow 57tr; G. Brad Lewis 103tl; Library Of Congress 95crb; Lockheed Martin Corporation/NASA 2-3; Jerry Lodriguss 21t, 77tc, 78-79, 106fbl, 107cl; Jean Lorre 64clb; Andrew J. Martinez 63ca, 63cra; Max-Planck Institute for Radio Astronomy 12l; Robert Mcnaught 78cl; Peter Menzel 13br; Allan Morton/Dennis Milon 16cla, 109t; MSSS/JPL/ NASA 51fcrb, 65cr; David Nanuk 10l, 13l; NASA 26r, 37cr, 38fclb, 46clb, 55cra, 64bl, 66-67c, 87tl, 107fcra, 111cl, 120br, 122; NASA/ ESA/ STSCI/Hubble Heritage Team 65bc; NASA/JPL/Space Science Institute 107fbr, 121crb; National Optical Astronomy Observatories 102-103; David Nunuk 5cra, 12c; Walter Pacholka-Astropics 80ca; David Parker 11r, 92c; David Parker-ESA/CNES/Arianespace 31bc; Physics Today Collection/ American Institute of Physics 97cr; George Post 55l; Ria Novosti 30clb, 38clb, 43cla, 120bl, 120cr (moon), 120fcla, 120fclb; Paul Robbens & Gus York 33br; Royal Observatory, Edinburgh 15bl; Royal Observatory, Edinburgh/AAO 5crb (nebula); John Sanford 28-29t, 107tc, 110-111 (moons), 111fbr; Friedrich Saurer 13bl, 15tr, 34tr, 36bl, 40cb, 42bl, 48c, 56cb, 64ca, 67tr, 81cra, 91tc, 97br, 104cb, 111ftr; Jerry Schad 106-107 (b/g), 107ftr, 109c; K. Sharon/Tel Aviv U./NASA/ESA/STSCI 22-23c; Dr Seth Shostak 89crb, 92-93c; Eckhard Slawik 107tl; SOHO/ ESA/NASA 51ftr, 53c; Sheila Terry 78bl; US Geological Survey 56-57t, 65fcrb; Detlev Van Ravenswaay 5cr, 20-21l, 50-51, 51fcr, 65cb, 70-71, 81tr, 83cra; Victor Habbick Visions 90-91tc, 94-95; Richard J. Wainscoat, Peter Arnold Inc. 78br; F. Winkler, Middlebury College, MCELS Team/NOAO/AURA/NSF 15br; Frank Zullo 116bl. **Still Pictures**: Astrofoto 95bl. **STScI**: J. Bedke 9tr. **TopFoto. co.uk**: 94clb; Fortean 90bl; Ria Novosti 120clb.

All other images © Dorling Kindersley
For further information see:
www.dkimages.com

Acknowledgements
Dorling Kindersley would like to thank: Jon Woodcock for his invaluable guidance, patience, and humour; Peter Bull for artworks; Hedi Gutt and Clare Harris for design assistance; Fleur Star for compiling the index; and Alex Cox, Deborah Lock, and Zahavit Shalev for editorial assistance.